MW00424582

Praise for *The Definition of Success:*
What Living Homeless Can Teach You

"We need more entrepreneurs engaging the most difficult challenges our society faces today with these kinds of innovative businesses and approaches."

—Brad D. Smith, Chairman and CEO, Intuit

"It's critical that Christianity discovers ways to make the Gospel practical in a culture that changes so rapidly it's impossible to keep up. This book does just that, telling a story that is both inspiring yet relatable so that anyone—regardless of belief system—can say, 'wow, I'm not sure if I believe in Jesus, but there's something to this, and we need more of it.'"

—Richard Rohr, O.F.M.

"The Definition of Success thoughtfully examines areas of life that most of us leave unchallenged while pointing to a higher ideal that goes far beyond that of any political party. The truth of Jesus for Christians points to a way and a life, but this book helps give that message a universal meaning."

—Mike McCurry, Press Secretary for President Clinton

"This book says that our lives are about more than the way we conventionally define success or failure. When we look, we can find value in every story."

—Mark Sanford, U.S. Representative for South Carolina's 1st Congressional District

"This book tells an ordinary story with national significance. Its spirit captures the essence of what every city should be, a place where all citizens strive for the harmony and wellbeing of the city regardless of race, religion, socioeconomic status, politics or sexuality; a place where citizens, having seen one another's pain, do not walk by with indifference but overcome their fears to heal one another because it is right and true. This book captures the idealism of a city that is yet to come, that we can only strive for, and yet remains worthy of our striving."

—Mayor Joseph P. Riley Jr.

"The Definition of Success illustrates what all successful organizations should inspire: Find a Purpose worth total commitment of yourself (Heart, Soul, and Mind), while creating value to the community to sustain itself."

—Byron Davis, CEO of Fisher Price

"When I dream, I wish for the world in which there are many Derek Snooks whose eyes see the possibilities for those in need and in doing so find great purpose. Let's join hands with Derek to further his vision."

—Mayor John Tecklenburg

The Definition of Success:

What Living Homeless Can Teach You

Derek Snook

To those seeking purpose more than success.

Contents

Author's Note

The events in this book are true to the best of my ability compiled from memory, e-mails, journals, and follow up conversations. All names have been changed to protect the privacy of the people in this book, with the exception of a few nicknames.

The Purpose of This Book

During the year I voluntarily lived homeless, I learned a new definition of success—it is a life of purpose. My hope is that this book will help you do the same.

In this book, I refer to the old form of success as "success." I refer to this new definition of success as "purpose."

I learned that success is the ongoing process of three distorting and misleading ingredients. The first is self-preservation/self-help. The second is isolation. The third is stressfully guiding ourselves through culture-driven plans for our lives.

I learned that purpose is the ongoing process of three restorative ingredients.[1] The first is self-abandonment through helping others (best when a set project). The second is a community of unconditional love. The third is having a guide.

Success and purpose are lenses through which we see the world, shape our perceptions, and drive our action or lack of action. Because they are matters of the heart, they can even look the same. But they are not the same. They have opposite motives. They have opposite ends. Success promises life but ends in death. Purpose leads through death but ends in life.

Living homeless taught me a lot. I learned that in order to live I must flee success and cling to purpose. This is the story of that year.

Prologue
Moving In

"There's a demon living inside of me."

I met Walter on June 1, 2009, the day I decided to voluntarily live homeless. I moved into The Good Samaritan Mission where twenty-six men lived in the same room.

Walter was in his early thirties and had dark, curly hair. He was wearing a white t-shirt. He sat in a chair behind the Mission, smoking a cigarette. Walter told me he worked in the stock room at Victoria's Secret. He also said he'd been to prison once or twice. Then Walter added that a demon lived inside of him, as casually as he might mention going for a walk.

Walter often came to church with me. One time, my church's pastor prayed, "God, you are so great."

Walter responded out loud, so that people turned around and looked at us, "No, you are not." Then he got out of his seat and walked out. I followed him outside.

Walter began to cry. He told me through sobs that he'd invited the devil into his life while leading music at a church. He had a wife. She was pregnant. At the same moment his

1

wife gave birth to a stillborn, he learned the child was not his. The child belonged to another leader in the church. His wife left him. The church fired him. One night he started a fire, burned all his Bibles, and asked the devil to enter his life.

That first day on the back porch, Walter suddenly stopped the conversation. "You know, Derek, you aren't the typical person that lives at The Good Samaritan Mission. What are you doing here?"

I shifted in my seat. I gained a sudden interest in the grass in front of us. I stared at it. I imagined this demon-possessed man killing me right then and there with his bare hands. I thought about lying. I thought about insisting I couldn't afford anywhere else to live or that I had a history of drug and alcohol abuse. But that didn't seem right. Instead, I told Walter the truth. "I want to see what it's like living here and how I can help."

Walter turned and looked at me. He scrunched his eyebrows. He flicked the ashes off the end of his cigarette and put his hands on the arms of his gray plastic chair. He looked straight ahead.

"Walter," I said nervously, testing the waters, "what do you think people living in places like The Good Samaritan Mission really need?" I expected Walter to say a nice place to live, a job, or a good education. Instead, Walter told me what was obvious, something even a demon-possessed man knew.

He turned and looked me in the eyes. "All anybody really needs is hope," he said, then put out his cigarette and left the porch.

I sat alone. I looked at the Mission's van, at the lawn and the men drinking on the front porch across the street. All anybody really needs is hope. Did hope mean more than having a nice place to live, or a job, or a good education? And if so, then why had I spent my life chasing success? Things like a great job, a solid education, a family, and a nice house in a nice neighborhood? Needing answers to these questions was partly why I was where I was.

I wondered that day if, with hope, I could move through any circumstance. And if, without hope, my circumstances did not matter. If that was true, then Walter's and my shared need for hope meant we were equal. If that was true, it also meant some of the things I'd learned about Walter, myself, and success were lies.

Chapter One
Growing Up

I was four years old when my grandpa came to visit. He called me over to where he sat and placed his big hands on my shoulders. He wore a checkered button-down shirt with a pocket over the chest and a John Deere hat. He asked, "Derek, what do you want to be when you grow up?"

This was the first time anybody had wanted to know. I straightened my back, pulled back my shoulders, and told him, "Papa, when I grow up, I want to be a Teenage Mutant Ninja Turtle." I loved Teenage Mutant Ninja Turtles. I loved that Donatello, Michelangelo, Leonardo, and Rafael were a team. I loved that they ate pizza and didn't clean up. I loved that they fought bad guys. They stood for something. They protected their city, and they risked their lives to do it. Plus, I had a crush on the reporter.

"You can't be a Teenage Turtle," my Papa told me. He took his hands off my shoulders.

"Teenage Mutant Ninja Turtle," I corrected him.

"Whatever the name is, you can't be it."

"Why not?" Until this point I thought I understood what

really mattered when making these decisions.

"Well, for one thing," my Papa said, "Teenage Turtle—"

"Teenage Mutant Ninja Turtles!"

"For one thing," my Papa continued, "they don't get paid well. And for another, they don't have health benefits. And good luck getting your mother to let you live in a sewer!"

I listened intently and dropped my head to the floor, feeling shame at disappointing my Papa. My Papa put his hand under my chin. Our eyes met.

"It's okay, buddy," he assured me, as if he'd discovered the cure to my rare disease. "You could be an architect or an attorney or an engineer. You could sell insurance or real estate!" My Papa named these professions as if they were far more exciting than fighting bad guys with nunchucks.

"What's insurance?" I wondered.

We decided I would put some thought into it, and when he visited again, I'd have a new answer.

The next time my Papa visited, he called me to where he was sitting and, placing his big hands on my shoulders, asked again, "Derek, what do you want to be when you grow up?"

I'd noticed every few days a truck would come around the neighborhood with guys hanging on the sides. That looked like a lot of fun. The truck would stop, and the guys would hop off and grab containers and empty them into the back of the vehicle. These men were very kind because they did it for everyone in the neighborhood. I straightened my back, pulled back my shoulders, and declared, "Papa, when I grow up, I want to be a garbage man!"

Papa took his hands off my shoulders. He exhaled loudly. "Oh boy," he said under his breath. Pressing his hands on his thighs, he yelled to my mother, "Jeanette!" He stood up tall as a giant. "We need to talk!"

———

Our family lived in a small neighborhood on a cul-de-sac with a pond behind our house. In the pond lived a six-foot alligator. We had a small backyard with a wooden fence and a swing set.

My father was a preacher. He was thin with tan skin. He had red hair and freckles like me. He taught me to shoot a basketball in our driveway. He never corrected me when I shot left-handed even though I was right-handed. I shot while he mowed the lawn, hardly ever shooting high enough to hit the rim.

We played together most nights—basketball and what my dad called "horsing around." We wrestled and chased each other through the house. Once when we were horsing around, my father held me on the ground and tickled me. I laughed and kicked and broke one of his ribs. "Ouch!" he squealed. I started to climb on top of him. "Hey, Derek, hop off," he said, his face turned as he held his side. Then he added, "I think Daddy's hurt."

No matter the circumstance, what I had done or not done, my father always told me, "Derek, I love you just because you are my son."

———

One time I found a goose egg in our backyard near the lake. I knew a baby goose would come from that egg if I didn't touch it, and a baby goose would die if I did. I wanted to see what was inside. I found a stick. I broke the egg. I threw the stick down and ran inside.

Before bed, I told my cousins what I'd done. They were six and seven years old. They visited from Ohio and slept on the top bunk. The lights were off except for my Teenage Mutant Ninja Turtle nightlight. "Derek," they said, "if you do bad things without asking Jesus into your heart you will go to hell."

I pulled my Sesame Street blanket to just below my eyes and stared at the nightlight.

"You don't want to go to hell, do you?" they asked, their light blonde hair hanging in their faces as they leaned over the top bunk to look down at me.

I'd had a nightmare of hell before. In it, I saw two images. One was a dark street except for a single lamp hanging from a telephone pole. There was debris and graffiti. A man had his hands against a brick wall with his legs spread. Other men in cars drove by and shot guns at him. In the other image, people ran through a cornfield towards a church. They ran through rows and rows of corn with their legs and arms pumping, the children in front, the adults turning to see who followed. They slammed the doors to the church shut and placed a bar on the door.

"I don't want to go to hell," I pleaded.

"Then repeat after me," my oldest cousin said. "Dear Jesus, I know I'm a sinner...." And so I did. "What were the words again?" She asked my younger cousin.

"It's 'Please come into my heart and keep me,'" my younger cousin suggested.

"It's 'save me'!" my older cousin abruptly corrected her.

"That's it!" I exclaimed. "Saaaaaaavvee me!"

I said what they said, afraid of missing a word.

———

For my fifth birthday I asked for a Teenage Mutant Ninja Turtle sandbox. Instead, my Papa bought me a GI Joe Jeep that charged on a battery. It flew around our driveway and cul-de-sac at speeds up to five miles per hour.

"Derek," my father said, "you can drive it around the cul-de-sac but you cannot, I repeat, you cannot drive it down by the lake." I nodded my head with my arms at my side. "There's an alligator that lives in there," my father continued, "and the lake is deep. You could drown."

A few days later my father came home and walked through our backyard towards the lake.

"Derek," I heard. My heart immediately sank. I looked up. My father stood in front of me. His hands grabbed his hips. The sun began to set. "Derek," he said, "what are you doing down here?"

"Nothing." My hands clenched the back of my Jeep. I tried to pull it out onto the bank.

"How did your Jeep get in the lake?" he asked.

"It drove itself down here," I answered.

My father sent me to my room. He and my mother had a lengthy discussion. I turned the lights off and waited. I knew I had disobeyed my father.

Then he came in. He sat on my bed with his elbows on his knees and his hands clasped, leaning forward.

"Derek," he said, "I do not want to do this, but I have to give you a spanking." My father unbuckled his belt. "I'm giving you a spanking for driving your jeep down by the lake when I told you not to. You could get yourself hurt or drown down there," he continued, pulling the belt through the last few loops.

Before I could even protest I was bent over his knee. "If you're good, I'll give you only three spankings. If you aren't good, I'll give you four."

I held my legs together with my arms grasping the bottom my father's thigh. I stared at my bedroom door. The doorknob was gold and shiny.

Wack! I felt the burn on my rear end.

Wack!

Wack! It was over.

My eyes swelled and began to water.

I turned around. I looked up. Tears ran from my father's eyes. They streamed down his cheeks. He wiped his nose and pulled his shirt to his forehead. I wondered if my father had missed me and hurt himself.

"I'm sorry, Derek," he started to say. I threw my arms around my father's neck. I burrowed my curly red hair into his chest.

"It's okay, Daddy!" I said as I kissed his cheek. "It's okay! I'm not going down by the lake again."

———

As a child, I learned there were two ways to live, for success or for purpose. My cousin's way was success. It regurgitated a mechanical formula of right things to say and do, but it felt more like an insurance policy— like something my papa suggested I might sell one day. My father's way was purpose. Mysterious, simple, and costly—it helped me unlearn my cousin's lesson. And it worked. Though I occasionally carried on in my disobedience, I didn't want to. Not because I was afraid of my father, but because I knew he loved me and that his will was best.

My father could not see me in pain without feeling pain himself. And to this day, I can't imagine as a child seeing him cry without crying myself.

Chapter One Questions:

1. Even as children, we are born with the desire to do important things in the world that matter and in some way benefit humanity. When you were a child, what was it that you wanted to be when you grew up? Why? Don't worry if it's hard for you to remember, but it's worth trying.

2. What memories, good and bad, strike you most about your childhood before ten years of age? Can you see how those moments can teach you something meaningful, both good and bad?

3. What do you think of my childhood dream of hell? One image pictured social upheaval; the other pictured Christianity's retreat and seclusion from the rest of society.

4. My father's actions taught me that righting a wrong cost something. His love meant that he felt my pain. Whose wrong do you want to right so much that you are willing to feel his or her pain?

Chapter Two
The Missions

I attended a small, private college in Greenville, South Carolina, called Furman University, a school with students from mostly middle- to upper-class backgrounds. We commonly referred to campus as "the bubble" because hardly anybody knew what happened outside it. One time a friend and I decided, "We need to go help somebody and *do something that matters*." We drove downtown. I saw a guy biking across the street. He had a long beard.

I rolled down my window. "Hey, um…" I stammered. He stopped his bike and turned towards me. "Could I buy you a meal or something? Do you need some new clothes?"

His head jolted back. His face scrunched up. "Don't judge a book by its cover," he scoffed. He put his feet back on the pedals.

I rolled up my window, made a U-turn, and drove back to campus.

Spring Break of my junior year came. Everybody else had plans to go to Cancún. I had plans to do nothing because I was broke. Two days before Spring Break, I ran into my friend Aaron. We met during our freshman year and shared a house with seven other guys during our sophomore year. Aaron said that he and some people from a Christian organization on campus were headed to Boston for a week. They planned to stay at the Boston Crisis Mission.

"Is that like a homeless shelter?" I asked.

"Yeah," Aaron said, "it is."

"How much does the trip cost?"

"Two hundred dollars, and you're on your own for food," he replied.

Two hundred dollars was at the high end of my Spring Break budget.

———

By my junior year I'd already quit going to church and having anything to do with Christian organizations.

I grew up in my father's church, where people could recite by group who was going to heaven and who was going to hell. Christians were mostly going to heaven, with the exception of Catholics who, along with everybody else, were going to hell. We had a list of things to do to prove you were like Jesus: don't drink, don't have sex outside of marriage, vote republican, attend anti-abortion rallies, don't go to movies, listen only to certain kinds of music, don't curse, come to church on Super Bowl Sunday, and support American wars unconditionally. This was how we could tell the real Christians from the fakers.

I saw value in much of what I was taught at my church, but the things we made our primary rallying cries were a far cry from Jesus who said the greatest commandment was to "love God with all your heart, soul, and mind, and love your neighbor as yourself."[2] Jesus's interpretation of "neighbor" seemed to mean every beating heart.

After sermons when everybody else had left, I would go see the pastor. He sat behind a big desk in a small office with green carpet and a small window. On his desk was a picture of my mom wearing red lipstick, big earrings, and a black leather jacket.

The pastor was always happy to see me. I would climb into one of the two chairs facing him. "Dad," I would ask, "there's another church down the street. Why do all the black people go to church there and all the white people go to church here?" I wanted to know. "Dad," I would ask, "if all I have to do to go to heaven is say some magic words and follow some rules, why did they make the Bible so long? Why not just write the magic words and rules on the front cover to make it as easy as possible for everyone?"

As a child, I quietly noticed the occasional visitor with long hair who sat in the back. One church member would approach to say "hello" while everybody else moved a little closer together and checked for their wallets.

I quietly listened as one church member would whisper about another whose family member was same-sex attracted. "We need to pray for them," they always concluded.

What if Jesus showed up as someone with long hair or as someone who was same-sex attracted, just to see if we were loving people well in his name? He probably left our church, and many others, disappointed and angry.

It felt like our church cared more about its list of rules than it cared about its neighbors. Other than an annual canned food drive for the homeless, we did little for those Jesus cared about: the hungry, the weak, the orphans, the refugees, the poor, the widows, and those whose lifestyles and beliefs made them ostracized by society. At my church it felt—though it would have never been said—as though people struggling in life needed to get themselves together and then come to Jesus, even though Jesus treated people the other way around.

As I grew up, I wasn't willing to bail on my faith because of the authentic love I saw in my parents. Even though church members wouldn't have liked me going to movies and high school dances, my mom secretly let me go, and my dad turned the other way. Even though our church seemed to keep the needy away, the one day my father came home late from work was every Tuesday, when he spent time counseling inmates and leading Bible studies at Sheriff Al Cannon Detention Center.

Plus, I'd done my own research. I read the Bible while my dad preached. Jesus called the religious of his time hypocrites. That's interesting, I thought. Jesus said the religious put heavy burdens on the shoulders of others without even lifting a finger to help. He said that many will call him "Lord, Lord," but he never knew them.[3]

Instead, he knows those who do the will of his father. He said these people were evident by their fruit: love, hope, peace, patience, perseverance, humility, gratitude, and courage. He said good fruit could come only from a good tree.

I also noticed that when Jesus met people, he did not tell them to abandon their religious tradition but instead told them to follow and believe in him. C.S. Lewis, author of *The Chronicles of Narnia*, said, "We do know that no man can be saved except through Christ; we do not know that only those who know Him can be saved through Him."[4] Based on my middle school theological research, I agreed. I believed that everyone who calls on the name of Christ will be saved, but not everyone who calls on him calls him by name. It seemed to me that those who actually knew Jesus were a much broader group than what our church thought, extending across all faiths and belief systems, and at the same time much narrower—having nothing to do with theology or obeying a list of rules or saying a mechanical prayer. It actually required giving up all of that. As I quietly looked around my father's church while he preached, I thought, oh no. I wondered, does Jesus both complete and wreck every belief system, including the legalistic Christianity at my father's small church?

During my junior year, after my dad initiated changes to the church music, the Christians mutinied. Church members asked for donations back. People whom my family had been friends with for my entire life turned their backs on us.

My father called me before Fall Break. "Derek, it might be best for you to not come home," he said, his voice cracking over the phone. My father resigned without another job lined up. I worried about how my family would make ends meet. Then my father took a job that required my mom and little sister in middle school to relocate five hours from home.

I'd had enough. I began going against the "Christian" rules my church had set out, even the ones that had some merit. I became hostile towards Christianity.

But the things I read in the Bible while my dad preached stayed with me. They suggested that Jesus wasn't the problem. The Bible suggested that Jesus contested those who say they follow him while they secretly hijack him for their own power and superiority agenda.

Before I abandoned my childhood faith, I decided that I would engage Jesus directly. If he was hogwash like the other things I'd seen at church, I was going to toss my faith out the window.

As I weighed out Aaron's proposal for Spring Break, I felt the need to sincerely and honestly explore Jesus and come to my own conclusions. I saw this as a way to do so. I felt drawn by Aaron's effort to love others at the Boston Crisis Mission. And I'd always wanted to visit Boston.

———

Before we left, I wrote in the pollen on the back of the van window, "Compelled to love." Yet, even as we drove, I gazed out the window wondering how I'd make money when I graduated. The beaches of Cancún had too much sun for my ginger skin; but the metaphorical beaches of Cancún, the pats on the back, the social media posts, and the wealth that came with the ability to travel, were things I desperately wanted. We arrived in the city the next day, settled into the Boston Crisis Mission, ate at an Ethiopian restaurant, and went to bed.

Each morning, we walked to the historic Park Street Church, next to the Boston Common, where we met together as a group, recounting the day before and planning for the next. While I enjoyed our group, it felt like my cousin's prayer formula or an insurance sales meeting to discuss how close somebody we had just met was to committing their life to a certain faith.

"I had a really good conversation with so-and-so," someone would say. "I think he's close to giving his life to Jesus." While many of these conversations were as close to authentic as possible, and well-intentioned, they reminded me of times growing up when I scared several of my friends into "asking Jesus into their hearts." I'd have conversations with them in a booth at Chick-Fil-A, or late at night during a sleepover, or in my family's garage before a bike ride. It was always the same conversation my cousins had had with me. It started with, "You don't want to go to hell, do you?" Turns out, not many people do. It ended with repeating the magic words. The more I heard it, the more I suspected the people providing the mechanical formulas, myself included, too often missed the point to begin with. Worse, they suggested to those who repeated their words that they were going to heaven for reciting the mechanical formula, too.

Other things at the Boston Crisis Mission were energizing, like seeing an angry staff member and resident yell at each other or listening to a young man just a few bunks over from me play an amazing guitar.

I felt strangely at home among the homeless. These were people without walls and fronts and barriers to who they really were. Because what you saw was what you got, I felt no need to pretend myself. I laid in my bed, reading and feeling a sense of belonging, that I fit in.

One of my fraternity brothers had interned at the Boston Crisis Mission the previous summer. After we left Boston, when Spring Break ended, I asked if I could intern there the following summer. Unfortunately, they said I wasn't "mature enough." I followed up with an angry e-mail to prove their point.

———

When I graduated from Furman in June of 2008, I moved to Charleston, South Carolina. I worked as a tour guide to pay off my student loans. I had always noticed a small green sign as I drove down Meeting Street, and one day in November of that same year, I decided to pull in.

The Good Samaritan Mission was founded as a halfway house for homeless men in 1904. It had twenty-six beds and lockers in a dorm room. I asked the pastor (also the executive director) if I could volunteer. A few minutes later, I was armed with cleaning supplies for the dormitory, bathrooms, and showers—I'd never cleaned my own dorm, bathroom, or shower. Manny, the house manager, likely had to scrub, sweep, or wipe the places I accidentally missed. Then Manny told me to rake the leaves. I went outside and struggled to get the leaves into the bag. One of the guys drinking on the front porch across the street came over to help me.

"Give me the rake," he said, extending his hand towards me.

He moved the bag next to the pile of leaves. He placed a

foot inside the bag on each side. He leaned over the pile and began raking leaves between his legs, straight into the bag. "Like this," he said to me as if I were a child. I followed his advice and quickly became an expert at raking and bagging leaves for The Good Samaritan Mission.

I came back to volunteer three more times. The last time the pastor and I were standing in front of the Mission when I asked, "Hey, pastor, this may sound a little weird." I wasn't quite sure how to put my question. "I'm going to Kenya for four months, and I was wondering…" I said, pausing for a second. "I was wondering if it would be okay if when I got back I could live here? You know, if you'd let me? Maybe just for the summer before I go to graduate school?"

The pastor was a tall, fit man with wavy hair and blue eyes. He was a German Lutheran from Wisconsin. He wore a perfectly ironed shirt and pants.

The pastor tilted his head to the side with his hands on his hips. He studied me. "What do you mean 'live here'?" he asked. "Here at the Mission with the men?"

"Yes, here at the Mission with the men," I said.

"Why do you want to live here?"

Part of me felt a nagging desire to live at The Good Samaritan Mission. It was the same voice that nudged me towards the Boston Rescue Mission. The rest of me thought I was crazy. I asked the pastor, expecting to get a clear "No." Then I could put the idea to bed. I could feel like I had done what I could. A clear "No," however, isn't what I got.

"To see what it's like and if I can help," I answered as best as I could.

I could see the pastor mulling it over. It was a crisp autumn day in Charleston, a few weeks before Christmas, when the temperature outside did not require a jacket. The pastor kept thinking. I began to wish I'd never asked. I worried I might be unqualified as an intern staff member at a Mission but right on par as a resident. I hoped the pastor would tell me this was the worst idea ever, or just say no, or even, "Why don't you go home and think about it?"

Pointing his index finger at me, he said, "Sure. Come back from Kenya, and if we have an open bed, it's got your name on it."

Chapter Two Questions:

1. Living at the Boston Crisis Mission offered perspective on the needs of humanity. What opportunities from your past have given you perspective on the needs of humanity? What opportunities do you need to take in order to gain perspective?

2. I nearly missed out on a great opportunity traveling to Boston because of a group stereotype. Have you ever missed out on a great opportunity for the same reason?

3. Asking the pastor if I could live at The Good Samaritan Mission was a nagging question that wouldn't go away for me. It represented my next step. What nagging question that you need to ask might represent your next step?

Chapter Three
Kenya

From January to April of 2009, I volunteered at a school for orphans called Mbita Christian Academy (MCA) in Mbita, Kenya, a small fishing village on the shores of Lake Victoria. My father met Mike, one of the missionaries at MCA, while Mike was back home in the United States.

Yes, I thought I could help people. But I also wanted an adventure, and I privately enjoyed how others thought I was such a great person for going. I was also astounded you could write letters and people would send you money to help!

Additionally, I hoped living in Kenya would help me get accepted to graduate school to earn a PhD in history. Based on my research, if I published enough, I could make a good living. I planned to continue studying British missionaries in the context of nineteenth and twentieth century imperialism which was my focus in college.

Many British missionaries failed to distinguish being British from Christian. Kenyans, Indians, and others colonized by Britain described Jesus as someone who was white, spoke English, dressed British, and was very clean and tidy. Furthermore, if they said they believed in him, their children could get a free education. In some cases, the missionaries' failure led to tragic consequences including war and death.

Sam and Jess picked me up from the airport. After handling business for a few days in Nairobi, we drove for ten hours through the Rift Valley where we saw giraffes and Maasai shepherds on their cell phones, through rolling hills of coffee and tea farms in Kisi, and finally to Lake Victoria, a wide body of water with rising hills in an otherwise barren landscape.

Jess was from Texas. She had a tall, thin, elegant frame with freckles and light blue eyes and brown hair. She had a wide, playful grin. She moved to Mbita roughly twenty years earlier when she first saw the need to educate orphans in the area. She started MCA. Her courage roared like a lion.

She adopted two daughters, Ashanti and Ashanti, who she called Big A and Little A. Big A showed up on Jess's doorstep one night. Within the year, Little A had as well. The sisters were not biologically related. They attended a boarding school for missionary children outside of Nairobi, the cornerstone of which had been placed by Teddy Roosevelt. After showing up on Jess's doorstep as an orphan, Little A later received a scholarship to Vanderbilt University.

Sam also showed up on Jess's doorstep not long after Big A and Little A. He had a sturdy build with a sharp nose and a ponytail of brown and scattered gray hair. He worked construction in Tennessee before visiting Mbita on a mission trip. He flirted with Jess who, in her late thirties and running a school for several hundred orphans in Kenya, had no interest in flirting with a man from Tennessee. She told him to put up or shut up. Sam moved to Kenya, and he and Jess married. They had been married for eight years.

We pulled into Mbita, nothing more than dirt roads, trash, and a smattering of tin shacks for homes. We sat in a small yard while Jess visited a student. I sat in the backseat and looked at the trash in the yard.

We drove down a dirt road running parallel to the lake. Sam stopped the Land Rover. He spoke with a woman in broken English, Kiswahili, and Luo. She came from the other direction carrying a basin of water on her head. She wore a bandana on her head and a tattered but colorful blouse. She was barefoot. When we continued, Sam looked into the rearview mirror, his eyes making contact with mine. "Her son just passed away, Derek," he said. "I wanted to tell her how sorry we are."

We took a right on a downward-sloping dirt path with huge rocks and a few small tin and drywall homes along the side.

"Derek," Sam said, "can you hop out and open the gate?"

Jess pointed out all the flies. They formed a cloud around the gate and vehicle.

"It will be fine," Sam said, as if this were an initiation to life on the lake.

When the first European explorers came to Lake Victoria, they thought this exotic lake was on fire. They saw tall, thick clouds of smoke rising from it. The smoke, it turns out, was flies. When the flies made it to dry land they swarmed until they died. I swallowed many of them while opening the gate.

Missionary life was simple and difficult, but endearing. There was no running water or electricity other than a few battery-powered lights Sam and Jess sometimes turned on after dinner. We ate by candlelight most nights, and one of my chores was to wash dishes outside with a headlamp.

Once, Sam's flip-phone rang at dinner.

"Sam," I said, "do you want me to grab that for you?"

Sam looked at me across the table and smiled, the candlelight casting shadows on his face. Outside, I could hear the intermittent sounds of crickets and birds.

"Well, Derek," he replied, "I'm not a heart surgeon. I'm not the president. I'm not God. Nobody needs me that badly."

When it rained, water was caught in the catcher on top of the house and used for cold showers, which I took while standing in a bucket. The water in the bucket was then used to flush the toilet. There was a latrine as well where you could squat, but Sam said that "if you prefer a throne you could use the restroom inside the house." I did, though it was rather close quarters, and I worried Sam and Jess might get to know me better than they wanted to.

I slept in Big A and Little A's room while they were away at school. I sweated at night under a mosquito net, listening to waves as they crashed on the shore and the snorting of hippos; occasionally, I woke in the middle of the night to a drum circle.

At MCA, I assisted the fourth-grade math teacher and

tutored a small group of fifth-grade girls who had fallen behind on their multiplication tables. I also taught P.E. to the first- and second-graders. We played soccer almost every day, and my team always won even if I had to gently pick up a few children and move them to the side so I could score a goal.

Between these moments, I spent my time alone. I locked the door behind me at school and at home.

"Is everything okay?" Jess asked. She sat at her computer in the small office she and Sam used for administrative work at school. I stood in the doorway.

Life in Mbita was normal, but normal was hard. Conversations like the one Sam had with the woman carrying the water basin were common. I learned of multiple girls in the village, middle school-aged, who were impregnated by family members. I heard of mothers who prostituted themselves to provide for their children. Jess founded the school to support orphans, many of whom lost their parents to HIV and were born with the disease themselves. They accounted for roughly one in every four children at the school. They were just as lively as the others, just as active and laughed just as hard, but you could tell they were not well.

"I've never quite felt this way before," I said, "but I feel like I'm emotionally and psychologically breaking down." I stared at Jess blankly, unable to muster any kind of emotion.

I felt Sam and Jess keeping a concerned eye on me. "How are things today, Derek?" they would ask.

One Friday, I walked to the house from school a little

early. I grabbed an apple from a bowl on the dinner table and walked outside. By our gate I found a small group of children who should have been at school. They spoke Luo. Their bellies were swollen.

When they saw me, the entire group walked up. They reached through the gate with their hands open.

I thought about what would happen if I gave them the apple. They might argue and fight over it. Probably only the biggest one would eat it. Then they would all face the same seemingly endless line of difficulties.

I was not their provider. I could not sustain them. This was not a problem I could fix. I felt weak and ashamed. I felt helpless. I walked inside and sat in a rocking chair. I threw the apple core in the trash. And then I cried.

Chapter Three Questions:

1. Have you ever felt the responsibility to act in tension with that which is outside of your control? What's the balance?

2. "Many British missionaries failed to distinguish being British from Christian...In some cases, the missionary's failure caused tragic results including war and loss of life." Misguided intentions can do more harm than good. Have you ever seen someone or a group of people whose good intentions did more harm than good? What did you think about that? Have you ever been that person? Does hypocritical

action mean something is not true or that it's incredibly difficult to live up to the standard that is true?

Chapter Four
Martha, Martha

On a couple of occasions, Jess had me skip my normal day-to-day responsibilities at MCA and join Helen on home visits. Helen's job at MCA was in part to make sure the parents—and, in turn, the children—received the support they needed.

One Thursday, around 9 a.m., we walked down a dirt path off the main road. It was hot, dusty, and sticky. I focused on the back of Helen's shoes as I walked, trying to be as still as somebody walking in ninety-five-degree weather can be.

"I plan for us to visit two homes today," Helen said.

We walked with the lake to our right, up and over hills, for some time before coming to our first destination, the home of a first- and fifth-grader at MCA. We talked to their mother, a beautiful, sturdy woman. She had a strong jaw with a symmetrical face and a muscular body. Her feet were stubs—they had no bridges and no toes. This mother farmed more than an acre of maize.

Helen and I visited with her for over twenty minutes

before her co-wife joined us. The co-wives had been widowed. Helen and the co-wives spoke in Luo. There was a moment when both Helen and the co-wives were in tears. I sat in silence. They quietly cried for several minutes before Helen looked at me and said, "Derek, I admire these women. They are very strong." I nodded my head. I knew coming from Helen this meant something.

Helen looked at me as if to say it was time to go. We hit the dusty trail once again, and I followed along, staring at the back of Helen's shoes. Helen told me we had one more visit to make, but first she wanted to check on Old Momma.

We walked a few hundred yards or so, with the lake on our right, up and down a hill, along a winding path, through a series of large bushes, and into a clearing.

There were two huts. Nobody was home. Helen poked around and found a woman who called for the Old Momma.

"Just a minute," Helen said. "She's coming."

We waited for a few minutes. A woman unhooked a gate at the bottom of the hill, pulling the wire over a wooden stake. She had a child on her back and a *jembe*, or hoe, in her hand.

She climbed to the top of the hill and greeted us.

Old Momma had high cheekbones below her dark, narrow eyes. Her cheeks were concave and wrinkly. She was skinny. Her neck was strong with tendons galore. Beneath that was her shirt, bright ocean blue with scattered holes, hanging like a flimsy curtain from a piece of dental floss. Her skirt was colorful with a brilliant pattern of flowers, but it was dirty and torn. She didn't have shoes. She wore a thin wire for a bracelet and a shattered face on a watch that did not tick.

I gave her my hand. She took it in both of hers. She beamed a smile of gums and a few scattered teeth.

She invited us into her home. I ducked inside and took my spot in a seat by the door.

I had been in a lot of Kenyan homes. They were typically huts with walls made of mud and straw, dirt floors, and chickens running around inside.

Nearly every home had a picture of Jesus. One home had a picture of him next to a picture of the Blue Mosque in Istanbul. "What's that?" I asked. They told me it was Jesus. "No, the other picture." They didn't know.

"It's just nice," they said.

The Old Momma's home had a picture of Jesus hanging from his cross and a calendar from 2003 on the correct month even though it was 2009. The hut itself consisted of two rooms. There were chickens inside, and their chicks nibbled at my toes. The floors were dirty and so was the table. Of the two chairs, one had a cushion. The cushion was stained. Debris gathered in the corners. Small rays of light reflected off the particles of dust in the air.

The Old Momma had buried all four of her sons who one by one got "sick"—which was often a code for contracting HIV—and died. Then she raised the grandchildren they left behind. She outlived most of them, too. The one grandchild she hadn't outlived had a daughter and then left for the city. So the Old Momma raised her great-grandchild, now two or three years old, bright-eyed, innocent, and ready.

The little girl sat in the chair next to her great-grandmother. She played games and entertained herself. My eyes caught hers. I held them as long as she let me. She climbed in her great-grandmother's lap, then she stood. She pulled the thin wire on and off the Old Momma's wrist. The Old Momma rotated her wrist, trying to keep the little girl happy while she and Helen talked. At one point I asked Helen how old the Old Momma was. Helen asked in Luo and translated the Old Momma's answer. "Derek, she does not know how old she is."

As Helen and the Old Momma talked, the great-granddaughter began pulling down the top of the Old Momma's shirt, lower, lower, and lower. She let go and grabbed again, pulling even lower. Then she pulled just low enough that the skin darkened to a ring at the tip of a small supply of fat. I stirred in my seat. After a few seconds the Old Momma adjusted her shirt, never breaking eye contact with Helen.

Even in Kenya, thousands of miles from home, my mind distracted itself with a million different things. I worried about graduate school. I fretted over what I would do with my life. I thought about the girl I planned to ask on a date when I got back to the United States. I wondered whether she would say yes or no. I planned how I would make money one day. I thought about how wasteful it was to be insuring my car while it was sitting unused in my parent's driveway.

In the New Testament, Luke tells a story about cutting through distractions. The story is of Jesus' visit with Martha and Mary. In the story, Martha frantically cleans, cooks, and prepares the table in the kitchen. Meanwhile, in the living room, Martha's sister, Mary, is having a fantastic time with Jesus. In my mind, Mary resembles less of a grown woman and more of a child, laying on her stomach with her legs kicking in the air, wearing overalls and double ponytails with her head resting on her balled-up fists.

At first, Martha decides to suck it up. She mutters under her breath, "Somebody has to do something around here." Then she adds, "I've always been the responsible one." Finally, she concludes, "This is why Mary will never find a man or a job." But after spilling the flour, Martha's frustration gets the best of her. She slams the oven door, drops the cornbread, and flings off her apron. She storms into the living room, throws her hands in the air, points to her sister, glares at Jesus, and yells, "Tell Mary to help me!" Martha accuses not only Mary of wrong but also Jesus for not correcting Mary.

Jesus doesn't get angry or defensive with Martha. Nor does he correct Mary. Instead, Jesus endorses Mary's behavior. He tilts his head in a way only someone who loves Martha as much as he does could. He says her name twice, "Martha, Martha." Then Jesus gently tells her the truth, "You are worried and upset about many things, but few things are needed—indeed only one. Mary has discovered it, and it will not be taken away from her."[5]

Luke doesn't resolve the story for us. Luke doesn't say what Martha does next, if she yells, "I hate my life!" and storms back into the kitchen; or if she asks, "What's the one thing that matters!?"; or if she says, "Great! Let's order

Dominos!" and flings herself onto the couch. The story teaches that what really matters in life, purpose, is easy to find and often right in front of us; but it's even easier to be distracted from or to put off purpose until our many tasks are handled or until we're financially secure or until the kids are grown or until we retire or until we are dead.

As I thought about my distractions in that small mud hut in Kenya, I began to wonder which was more important: The Old Momma, a human being in need, or my troubles and problems and car insurance in the United States?

The early Christians would have said the Old Momma. They saw Jesus—based on his self-description—embodied not just in the Old Momma but in all of the poor. They kept an open bed with bread and a candle for the wandering Jesus who showed up at their door. They believed when someone like the Old Momma stopped in need it was as if it were Jesus himself. I wondered what the early Christians would think about my society, one where the rich lived too far away for the poor to ever reach?

The Old Momma and Helen continued to talk. After ten minutes of midday heat and untranslated Luo, my eyes became heavy. My head nodded. I wondered what the early Christians would say about a man who, with Jesus in front of him, fell asleep?

―――

"Derek, it's time for us to go," Helen said. I thought I heard something. "Derek, it's time for us to go," Helen repeated a little louder. I opened my eyes. The Old Momma sat with her hands in her lap. She smiled at me. The little girl sat on the floor.

We walked back up the dirt path, through the bushes, up and over the hill. When we got to the main road Helen looked at me. "Derek, the Old Momma is going to lose her land." She said it as if it were a matter of fact.

"What do you mean she's going to lose her land?" I asked, raising my voice.

"She said her neighbors have filed a land dispute against her," Helen replied calmly. "They will give five or ten dollars to the land official who will give them the Old Momma's land."

I stopped in my tracks. "What!?" I exclaimed. "That doesn't make sense, Helen. You can't just give somebody five or ten dollars and take someone's land!"

"It happens sometimes," Helen said. She started walking again.

"Where will she and her great-grandchild go?" I asked, opening my arms where I stood as Helen continued, walking with her back to me. She turned and looked over her shoulder.

"She doesn't know, Derek."

"What can we do to stop it?"

"Nothing," Helen said. "Come on, Derek. We need to go."

I didn't help the Old Momma that day. I mentioned it to Sam and Jess and then did nothing. I could have done something. I could have barricaded myself in the Old Momma's hut and contacted all of my friends in law school until I found an attorney willing to defend the Old Momma.

If I were someone speculating as to why I didn't help that day, I could come up with a lot of good excuses. Perhaps I had a very important meeting to help another Old Momma already on my calendar, or perhaps Helen said she would do something, or perhaps I simply felt overwhelmed or afraid. Perhaps I was inspired to go earn a master's degree and start a nonprofit about land rights issues in Kenya to get at the core of the problem instead of an individual case.

At the end of the day, Luke's story best explains why I didn't help. I flew halfway around the world in search of purpose to discover it was all around me before I stepped on the plane. Purpose is easy to find. It's in the face of every human, rich or poor, American or Kenyan. But even when it's directly in front of me, it's even easier to get distracted.

Chapter Four Questions:

1. Hearing the Old Momma would lose her land made me embrace the hope that "the last will be first, and the first will be last."[6] I wanted to see this Old Momma be among the first. Have you ever had a similar experience?

2. Injustices exist all around us. What injustices have you noticed? Which one would you want to fight against?

3. Over time, Christians institutionalized through charities the practice of keeping an open bed, bread, and candle for the wandering Christ in need. Early

critics thought that it was incompatible to be a Christian and send the wandering Christ to a charity instead of serving him yourself. What do you make of this?

4. "Purpose is easy to find. It's in the face of every human, rich or poor, American or Kenyan. But even when it's directly in front of me, it's even easier to get distracted." For me, doing nothing to help is one of the saddest things I've left undone. Do you see purpose around you? Are you distracted from it? How? Why?

Chapter Five
Promises and a Change in Plans

Most days at MCA I sat in the back of the fourth-grade math class. Despite being the teacher's assistant, the teacher never asked me to do much. I wrote in my journal instead. I wrote desperate prayers. "Dear God, please help me to figure out my life. I love you and I need you. Amen." When I wrote desperate prayers I would sometimes take a deep breath and feel tingling throughout my body. The prayers turned to incoherent scribble marks.

One day, looking out at Lake Victoria, I wrote: "Dear God, if you give me something meaningful and purposeful to do with my life, I won't quit until you say it is time to quit or until it is complete."

Within a week I began receiving e-mails from my dad regarding my graduate school applications. "Derek, I'm sorry," the first e-mail began. "We got letters from Penn and NYU today and they said you were not accepted. I'm sorry." Then a few days later I got another e-mail from my dad. "Derek, I'm sorry," it began. "We got letters from Harvard and Columbia today, and they said you were not accepted.

I'm sorry." It went on like this until there were no more schools left.

Every Sunday evening the missionaries would gather together for worship and prayer and popcorn or brownies. That evening we met at Jackie and Luke's. They had a son. They also adopted a Luo girl named Grace. They had a very small house that sat a couple hundred yards from Lake Victoria. I sat on a couch with Mike. The window behind us looked out at the lake. Luke sat in a chair in front of me to the right. Jackie sat next to him, across from us. Sam and Jess were out of town. We sang together while Luke played guitar. Then we shared prayer requests.

"I could use prayer," I said. "I've been rejected by all of these graduate programs, and I'm not sure what I'm supposed to do with my life." I didn't tell them about the promise I'd made in the back of the fourth grade math class. "I feel really scared," I said.

When it came my turn, I prayed, "Please, God, please help me figure out what you want me to do with my life. Thank you that I didn't get accepted." As I prayed I began to sob. I didn't want to, but I couldn't stop it. Everyone was looking at me. Given the circumstances in Mbita, graduate school didn't seem an appropriate thing to cry over. But they didn't judge. They sat and waited. Rays of light beamed through the window behind Mike and me. The sun set over Lake Victoria, sneaking behind a host of clouds.

I cried not only tears of sadness. I cried tears of joy.

I'd put an incredible amount of pressure on myself regarding graduate school. Finding out this wasn't possible released me to be me. I had no idea what that meant. But I felt free to not be on some straight and rigid path. I tried that path and it said, "No." I didn't see it as a coincidence that as soon as I made that promise I got answers.

I'd already decided to move into The Good Samaritan Mission. I decided when I ate the apple and felt helpless to make a meaningful difference for those children. I decided when Helen told me about how the Old Momma and her great-grandchild were losing their land, and I did nothing.

How could I be both ultimately helpless to do anything and yet responsible to do something? If I saw myself as being entirely helpless, I would lead a life of apathy and be forced to dig a hole in the sand to put my head in. If I saw myself as being entirely responsible, I would lead a life of anxiety, always panicking about whether or not I had done enough. Is one true and not the other? Could both be mysteriously true at the same time? Do we both accept the world as it is while we strive for a world that is not yet? Or was it neither? I wanted to know.

I felt how I answered these questions would affect the deepest parts of how I saw and lived life. Mbita taught me that I had to walk in the shoes of those who are different from me in order to understand their problems and answer these questions. It reaffirmed my father's lesson, that fixing another's problem was costly. It required feeling someone else's pain.

But I didn't need to come to Africa to find poverty and injustice. I could find it where I was from, the United States, in Charleston, South Carolina, where I already had the advantage of better understanding the culture and context.

I had been waiting to get accepted to graduate school to make the decision public. That way, when I said, "I've decided to live at The Good Samaritan Mission," I could quell concerns by adding, "It's just for the summer. Then I'm attending Harvard," or whatever. My misguided desires for approval and acceptance led me to focus on status and career and money. Service became a secondary way to gain even more approval and acceptance for being recognized as a good person. I wanted to manipulate generosity and service to feed my success.

But when my plan failed, The Good Samaritan Mission remained.

As I walked home from school a week or two later, I realized that if I actually cared about serving others I should move into The Good Samaritan Mission anyway. I walked down the dirt road headed toward Mbita and turned off to Sam and Jess's. I walked down the path and opened the gate.

Jennifer and Owen were living with Sam, Jess, and me at the time. Jennifer and Owen were from Portland, Oregon. They showed up in Kenya with their three adult children and no plan. They approached the Anglican Church in Nairobi who asked them all to come to Mbita, and so they did.

When I walked in, Jennifer sat at the dinner table. "Jennifer," I said, "it's official. When I get back to Charleston, I'm going to live in a homeless shelter." I expected a celebration. I expected a pat on the back. I expected Jennifer to be gung-ho.

"Why are you going to do that?" she asked. She listened patiently while I explained. "That's an interesting idea," she said, "but maybe you should think about it some more and decide when you get home."

But I'd moved past that place. I had made a decision. "Thanks, Jennifer," I said, "but I'm moving into The Good Samaritan Mission."

———

Lots of people asked me why I decided to live at The Good Samaritan Mission.

I gave them philosophical answers. I told them, "I need purpose." I paraphrased Thoreau, saying, "Most men live lives of quiet desperation, and I don't want that."

I gave them logical answers. I said, "When I was in Kenya, I felt a disconnect between those who want to help and those they are trying to help. I realized I didn't need to go to Kenya to find that problem. It exists where I am from with the homeless and those who want to help the homeless. The way for me to help is to empathize with them and walk in their shoes."

Those reasons affirmed the ongoing testing of my faith. I decided to move into The Good Samaritan Mission because if it is true that Jesus came from heaven to earth to relate to us and help us with our problems, and he is my example, then it only makes sense that I would try, even in the smallest and most insignificant of ways, to do the same for others.

I didn't want to say God existed with my mouth but

couldn't possibly exist with my action or lack of action. I didn't want to be like a salesman who sold Chevies when he drove a Ford. I wanted to grind faith against action. I wanted to see if it was real.

When I got back to the United States, I spent a few weeks with my parents in Asheville, North Carolina. I drove along the Blue Ridge parkway, parked my truck, and laid in its bed looking out at the mountains.

Despite my concern about not acting out my faith, I made a few last ditch efforts to do so anyway and avoid The Good Samaritan Mission. I applied to AmeriCorps but was rejected. I asked the girl I liked out on a date. She, too, said no, though very nicely. Had we started dating, I would have had good reason not to move into The Good Samaritan Mission.

Then I drove to Charleston. "You have to promise to kick me out after three days," I told my friends. "I'm going to move into a homeless shelter."

"Are you sure?" they asked. "You can stay here longer if you need to."

A few days later I drove down Meeting Street to the green sign that pointed to The Good Samaritan Mission. I put on my turn signal and slowed down. Then I sped up. I drove instead to the apartment I had stayed at one summer during college ten blocks away on Radcliffe Street. I sat with my sweaty hands clenched around the steering wheel while thoughts raced through my mind:

If I move into The Good Samaritan Mission my friends and family might think I am a loser. It won't be comfortable.

It might hurt my chances at a good-paying job. I could miss opportunities at graduate school. I could get sick in the Mission. It will be really awkward to bring a girl back to my place to watch a movie with a bunch of other homeless men. Will I be safe? What if the men at the Mission do drugs? What if they physically hurt me? How do I think I'm going to help them anyway? What do I know about their problems?

But how do I find purpose in my life? I have to know. What if purpose comes from helping others? And if so, then to what degree do I have to walk in their shoes to understand what they really need in order to help them? If I stay where almost everyone looks, thinks, and acts like me, how will I see the suffering of those who are different from me, experience their pain and walk in their shoes? This step seems like the only way for me to gain the experience needed to live and thrive—and to discover my purpose.

No matter how much I think about this, my reasoning will never bring me to a place of absolute certainty. And I don't want to lie on my deathbed thinking about something I wish I'd done. If I don't like it, I can move out so long as nobody murders me in my sleep. I have to try.

My hands were still clenching the steering wheel.

I took a deep breath.

Then I muttered, "Fine, let's do this." I started the engine. I drove down Meeting Street. I put on my turn signal. And I pulled in.

I met with the pastor. He explained the rules. No drugs or alcohol were allowed. On weekdays we had to leave by 7:30 a.m.

and could not come back until after 4 p.m. Curfew was 11 p.m. on weekdays and midnight on Friday and Saturday. Dinner was every day at 6 p.m. sharp. We had to attend worship services at the Mission at 8 a.m. on Sundays, even if we attended a different church. Every weekend, each of us had a chore to do: vacuuming, cleaning the bathrooms or kitchen, or mopping the floors. Rent was eighty dollars a week, due Friday by 5 p.m., and that included housing, utilities, and dinner.

The pastor took a picture of me with a Polaroid camera and pinned it to the board by the front door which displayed pictures of all of the men who lived at the Mission. I learned a few of their names: Walter, Gerald, Frank, Raul, and Bill.

Manny, the house manager, showed me my locker where I could put my things. He showed me the bed I would be sleeping on, a top bunk in a room with twenty-five other beds. "The guys who have been here the longest get the bottom bunks," he said. "I'll let you know when one comes available if you want it. Here are your sheets."

Chapter Five Questions:

1. Approval from friends, family, and society are normal motivations in our lives. Approval, I must confess, is one of my biggest struggles. Have you ever let the approval of others keep you from doing what you knew was the right thing or push you towards doing what you knew was the wrong thing? How could the approval of others discourage or encourage you to do something that matters?

2. Can you relate to the rejection I felt from my failed plan of graduate school? Have you ever had doors closed that pushed you from one direction towards another?

3. "How could I be both ultimately helpless to do anything and yet responsible to do something? If I saw myself as being entirely helpless, I would lead a life of apathy and be forced to dig a hole in the sand to put my head in. If I saw myself as being entirely responsible, I would lead a life of anxiety, always panicking about whether or not I had done enough. Is one true and not the other? Could both be mysteriously true at the same time? Do we both accept the world as it is while we strive for a world that is not yet? Or was it neither? I wanted to know." What do you think about this? Where do you think your responsibility for action ends and begins when it comes to helping others?

4. Living an authentic faith was significant motivation for my decision to move into The Good Samaritan Mission. What are significant motivations and values for you?

Chapter Six
About Love

Everybody hated Chip. I met him in the Mission's parking lot. He went to Alcoholics Anonymous next door. When I asked Chip where he lived, he responded with, "I live on the streets. I make money—that's what I do."

Chip was a pain in the butt. Nobody liked him. The men at the Mission didn't like him. Manny, the house manager, said, "He's trouble." One day, I came into the pastor's office, and he had a picture of Chip walking behind a car in his cut-off Michigan Wolverine sweater. Chip was average height with a beer belly and short, crew-cut hair. He had a dark complexion outlined by great tan lines that cut off at the upper biceps. The sun had prematurely wrinkled his face. His eyes were a light blue. Chip appeared to be in his early forties.

The pastor stood behind his desk with one hand on his hip and the other hand pointing down at the picture. "This guy is trouble," the pastor said. "He keeps breaking into the Mission's backyard and stealing things from our shed," he added, "but we can't catch him."

The pastor called the cops on Chip.

Chip would yell across the fifty-car parking lot the Mission shared with the small shopping center next to it. "Bo!" he yelled, bee lining towards me as I got out of my car. I kept my head down and pretended I didn't hear. I grabbed my book bag from the back seat. I looked up and Chip was next to me. "Hey, Bo!" Chip smiled at me as if we were brothers.

I gave Chip a weary look. I wasn't interested. I climbed into my car to get my things, hoping Chip would have moved on by the time I got out. Chip never budged. He took it as a sign of interest. "Hey, Bo, can you spare some change?" he asked with the friendliness of a man who was offering me a free meal.

If I said yes, I'd have to stop whatever I was doing to find change for Chip. "No, Chip," I said, "I don't have any cash on me." Before I could even finish, Chip interjected.

"Come on, Bo! Can't you spare a quarter?!" The second request was always louder than the first. "Come on, Bo! I'm just trying to get some money for food. Help a brother out!"

I leaned into my car to find some change under a seat.

"Making money," Chip would proclaim, "that's what I do!" Chip, as far as I know, did make money. He put a lot of hours into panhandling—more hours than he might have at a regular job.

Chip and the cops were on a first-name basis. The East Side neighborhood constantly called the cops to take Chip to prison. He'd be gone for a week here and a week there— public intoxication here, disorderly conduct there. Then he'd be back, as if the prison didn't want him either. It was a game of Chip, the Hot Potato.

When Chip wasn't taking trips to jail, he was taking them to the hospital. One time he was gone for a week and came back still wearing his hospital gown. He even had his wristbands on. I could see Chip hopping out of his hospital bed and walking out of the place. But really, where were his clothes?

"What were you doing in the hospital?" I asked Chip.

"Ah, Bo, somebody stabbed me," he said as if it had been a routine checkup.

"Stabbed?" It sounded a bit heavy even for Chip.

"Yeah, a guy stabbed me," he confirmed.

"Why?" Chip ignored the question.

"Have you seen Cindy?" he wanted to know. Chip was pacing. I thought he might walk away.

"Chip, I don't understand. Why did somebody stab you?"

"I haven't seen her since I went to the hospital," he continued, raising his hands and pacing back and forth.

Cindy had rosy white skin, red cheeks, and curly brown hair. She appeared to be in her mid-thirties. She was average height and very skinny. She wore a look of constant exhaustion. She had what I called "cottonmouth," a ring of white foam around her lips. Most of the time she stumbled around, wearing a long-sleeve sweater. She never wore a bra. She was always digging to the bottom of cigarette containers looking for a cigarette that hadn't been smoked all the way.

Cindy came to Charleston with a man, but when things fell apart, she ended up at the homeless shelter a few blocks from The Good Samaritan Mission. That's where she met Chip and his friends Jerry and Brock, waiting in line one evening to be let into the shelter. Chip said after Cindy moved into the shelter she began experimenting with cocaine.

"One night," Chip said, "I found Cindy in a bad state. She was all alone. She was strung out laying with her back against a fence. Her head was hanging on her shoulder. I held her. 'Everything is going to be okay,' I said. Then I went to my friend in the neighborhood. She makes food for me sometimes, green beans and collards and macaroni and cheese and pork chops. I knocked on her back door, and she turned on her light and gave me some. Then I brought it and a beer back to Cindy. 'Here' I said, 'drink this, eat this.'"

Chip recognized there was only so much he could do. "I want to get both of us off these — streets," he'd say. "People say if I get a better life for myself, then maybe she will follow." Chip sometimes attended the Alcoholics Anonymous next to The Good Samaritan Mission. I was pretty sure they gave him this advice.

Most of Chip's efforts to benefit his own life seemed to come from a desire to benefit Cindy's. And it would always send him backwards when she would "diss" him or he'd find her with another man or strung out on drugs. Chip loved Cindy. "Because of that smile," he said. "Yeah, it's because of that smile." He'd exhale, cracking one of his own. "It's my fault for falling in love."

I wanted Chip and Cindy to figure things out, get clean, work simple jobs, and take care of each other. They could be happy together, and they both deserved it. I mean, after all, Chip was willing to take a knife for her.

"That's how I got stabbed," Chip finally said. "Cindy and I were at the shelter and this guy was calling her names. I told him to cut it out, but he wouldn't. So we took it outside. The guy pulled out a knife. That was Tuesday."

It was Friday. Chip had been released and spent the day in a hospital gown roaming Meeting, King, and Columbus streets, asking if anyone had seen Cindy.

Weeks passed by. I saw Chip briefly once or twice. He'd finally learned Cindy had been arrested for slapping a police officer. "I'm not sure how long she'll be in for," he said, dropping his head towards the pavement. "I don't know if she'll ever come back."

The next time I saw Chip he was in front of the Alcoholics Anonymous building wearing an R.I.P. Michael Jackson T-shirt. He started with the usual, "I live on the streets. I make money—that's what I do. I make five dollars here and five dollars there. I live on the streets. I make money—that's what I do." But soon he began talking about Listerine Sam—Listerine being Sam's drink of choice— whom Chip had been accused of killing one night behind the Mission on Nassau Street. "They think I killed Listerine Sam, but I didn't," he said, his face reddening, throwing his hands in the air. "I didn't kill him!"

It had been a tough rumor for Chip to shake. I'd heard it from a couple of different sources, and it seemed to follow him everywhere he went.

Then he talked about Cindy. "She steals from me and

screws me over… I like to drink a little, but I keep thinking I can change her." Then he added again, "It's my fault for falling in love. I just know I can't keep living on the street."

Chip cared so deeply about his ability to make five dollars here and five dollars there. It gave him a sense of self-worth. That's what Chip meant when he would insist, "All these people respect me." It revealed a lot when he paused and then said, "…but I don't respect myself."

He tried holding himself up by talking about the things he had. "I got some money in my pocket…I got…I got…."

I interjected, reaching for anything, "You've got your mama, Chip."

"No," he said, "my mama's dead."

When I first met Chip, sitting on a park bench in Marion Square one night, he explained his mama was the only person in his entire life who ever stood up for him. When he was a kid and bigger kids would bully him, she'd come outside and run them off. He told me even though she was dead, he talked to her every night. He insisted she could see him, and he always pointed at the moon.

"I saw your mama this morning, Chip," I insisted. "I was driving to work and saw a full moon in the rearview mirror, and I thought, 'There's Chip's mama!'"

Chip started to cry. "You're right," he said, "I do still have my mama." Chip hugged me. His chin was bleeding a little and got on my shirt. My arms squeezed my side as he pulled me closer. He burrowed into my chest like a child. "I've still got my mama," he repeated and sobbed.

"Yeah, Chip, you've still got your mama," I said, looking over his shoulder and trying to breathe.

"I'm sorry. It's just that I've had a bad day. Jerry and Brock dissed me—they got a hotel. I want to get off these — streets and this — alcohol." Chip held me tight.

I looked around, knowing the guys at the Mission wouldn't like it if they saw me with him. I was a little embarrassed. But Chip really did need a good sob. He was still using my shirt as a Kleenex when Mattie came strolling by on his way to the Dollar General. Chip struck up a conversation. Mattie looked like a deer in headlights. He squirmed and asked Chip how long he'd been out of the hospital.

"Oh yeah?" Mattie stammered. "Well, you look good," he said. "I've got to go to the store." Mattie left, and Chip began to tear up again.

After a few minutes, Chip stopped crying. He pulled his shoulders back and began his normal banter. He wiped beneath his eyes and the scruff on his face with the back of his hand. I hung around, listening to him talk about the streets and Cindy.

"Will you buy me a pack of cigarettes?" he asked. Typically, I wouldn't have, but I planned to make an exception on account of Chip's rough day. "Here," Chip said, and pulled money out of his pocket to give me.

"What are you doing?" I asked, raising an eyebrow.

"They won't let me in there. Here," he added, "here's some for you, too."

"Chip, you don't have to do that," I said.

"Get yourself something. A Coke or something. Get me Red Marlboros."

When I came out, I handed Chip his cigarettes.

Chip began to tell me a story. One night, in 1989, he was at a bar outside of Columbia, South Carolina. A girl approached him to have sex with her. He hesitated at first, fighting the urge, and fixated instead on the beer in his hand. After a few more Miller High Lifes and more attempts by her, he ended up taking her to his place. She didn't tell him that she was underage. Her parents pressed charges, making Chip a sex offender. While I was unable to verify whether or not Chip's version of the story was true, I searched for him on the South Carolina sex offender registry a few days later and his face popped up.

Chip explained he couldn't get a job unless it was under the table or working day labor. Sex offenders can be denied any job, even ones without contact with women and children. That's why Chip panhandled so much. Sex offenders can be denied by landlords, and they can't live within a certain distance from schools. "They can't even stay here or at The Salvation Army or the homeless shelter because of the liability," the pastor told me once. "Sex offenders are the lepers of our day."

"What am I supposed to do except buy a half pint of liquor and find a spot and drink the night away?" Chip asked. "I'm just trying to be real with you, Bo. Everybody on the streets respects me, but I don't respect myself." I could see how, if I had done what Chip did, I might act the same way. I could feel his shame of making a bad decision that would never go away. Chip's entire life had been damaged by what sounded like an inadvertent mistake.

––––

Chip disappeared a few months later from his usual haunts: Upper Meeting, King, and Columbus Streets.

A few years later, when I'd moved out of The Good Samaritan Mission, one of the officers who worked the East Side neighborhood told me Chip died from cirrhosis of the liver.

Cindy hasn't left. I saw her the other day sitting on the sidewalk in front of AA and said, "Hey, Cindy! How are you?" She looked up and grumbled, "It's my birthday," and then dropped her head to stare at the pavement. The same officer told me Cindy's son even moved from another state to try to help her. Her upper-class family from New York came to one of Cindy's courtroom hearings in Charleston. The judge offered to let Cindy go home to her family who had a house purchased and waiting for her. Cindy responded, "I'm not going back with those people. I'm fine. I like where I'm at."

––––

After I learned of Chip's death, I thought more about our last conversation. I sat in Marion Square, the place where we first met.

I wrote in my journal: "I find meaning in that Chip, who crossed streets without looking while yelling at and stopping moving cars, who drank and slept in the streets, and who walked out of a hospital still wearing his gown, lived for so long. He had been holding on to something—a better life for himself and Cindy—and he was willing to sacrifice for it. But something else had sustained Chip, too. I think it was love."

That realization came as a relief because I secretly saw myself in Chip and Cindy. I roam the streets of life searching for what makes me whole. I agonize over mistakes I've made and things I've left undone. I medicate along the way, sometimes with alcohol, or quick validation, or a false superiority. Until Chip and Cindy, I thought receiving love required being physically attractive, put-together, smart, and funny with a good job and money in my bank account, or at least the appearance of it. Instead, I learned love that mattered became stronger with grit and mess.

It's like Chip always said, "I'm just trying to be real with you, Bo."

Chapter Six Questions:

1. Chip's story involved a mistake that haunted him the rest of his life. Have you ever done, said, or thought anything that you'll always wish you could take back?

2. Early on, I labelled Chip as a lazy drunk. By labelling, I dehumanized Chip to the extent it surprised me he could love and receive love. Learning more about his story helped me understand why he behaved the way he behaved. Who have you labelled? How might that

have kept you from understanding that person? Who has labelled you? How did you feel?

3. Jesus spent his time with society's most rejected individuals. Do you think sex offenders are on this list? Who else is on this list?

Chapter Seven
A Taste of Heaven

"Listen, listen," Tom, who we called Boston, began in a strong Boston accent. "I'll tell you what happened. Skip owned the bar, right? Well, Skip died and the bar closed down, right? Well, a couple months later, me and Pat were out back of the bar drinking, so we broke the door off to go in and have a drink. Pat says to me, 'Tom, let's just open the bar.' So I was working for Budweiser at the time, and that week I got twenty cases of beer. We ran electrical cords from a neighbor's power source and got the electricity going. We got booze and bartenders and everything. And that Saturday morning we opened. It was just like the show *Cheers*, 'where everybody knows your name!'"

———

Once, in eighth grade, I asked my friends, "Do y'all's dads have any friends?" We sat in the driveway between games of basketball.

One by one they answered, "No, not really." As kids, none of us could imagine life without our friends. Yet, our dads seemed to have none at all! "That's a sad thing to think about," Jason said, sipping on a Capri Sun.

While homelessness caused incredible pain, loneliness was one problem we never had, sleeping next to twenty-five other men. Every night, after work, the men would sit in plastic chairs out front of the Mission, smoking cigarettes and telling each other stories from their past, stories about exes and family. We debated politics and religion. We greeted our friends who showed up for meetings at Alcoholics Anonymous next door.

The men lived far more interesting lives than I could have imagined. Much of what was said I was able to verify. But the men seemed to know when somebody was completely making something up. Sometimes they contested it. Other times they simply went along, nodding their heads. They knew there's not a soul among us that doesn't wish some things to be true that aren't.

As I sat and listened, I wondered: If purpose came from helping others, didn't I need deep, long-lasting community to understand what people need and to be loved and supported by them? Weren't relationships the heartbeat of life? And why did failing at the American Dream seem to facilitate relationships more than succeeding at it? From what I could tell, from my vantage point at the Mission, the problem had two components.

For one, the neighborhoods in which my friends and I grew up limited, rather than created, interactions between people. Jane Jacobs, the famous urban planning journalist and activist, insists certain characteristics play heavy roles in creating communities that grow together and stay together: the layout of streets; walkability; access to affordable and diverse housing; integration of residential, commercial, and public spaces; and more. Our neighborhood was "handicapped by sameness." Jacobs warns, "Neighborhood accommodations for fixed, bodiless, statistical people are accommodations for instability."[7]

For another, my father and my friends' fathers played the role their society demanded of them. They were economic engines. Our fathers worked hard, even on weekends. They provided for their families. They loved their children and their wives. They were good dads and good men. They did not complain. How could they while sitting at the top of the American food chain? Each of them was a success.

But engines, it turns out, don't have friends.

Even as our fathers exercised the freedoms their society expected of them, they shut the door tight to their own loneliness. They became victims to places where people served economics. Instead, economics ought to create communities with exercise, life, margin, laughter, and, above all, relationships that serve people.

————

"Yeah, so we kept that bar for a little over a year," Boston continued in his Boston accent. Lebron, Walter, Lyrel, Daniel, and I sat on the front porch listening to Boston. "Did the front locks and everything! It was our bar! We'd have horseshoe tournaments in the summer time, dart tournaments in the winter. You know? There'd be fifty, sixty people in there. We never had a problem, not for a year! Then one day a construction company bought it and did the whole building over and we had to get out. Never heard a word from whoever was paying our electric bill!" Boston laughed. "It was our bar, yep, we opened it up. We were proud of that place. Made a ton of money. A ton of money!" I generally believed Boston's stories, my favorite of which was the time he told us about how he thought his "old lady," or girlfriend, a cop herself, had started cheating on him with another cop. The cop drove by one day in his police car, so Boston got in his own car and started chasing him. The cop immediately called for backup. I imagined Boston in a car chasing after one cop while other cops chased him. According to Boston, though, the cops never bothered him on account of his "old lady."

"Uh-huh," Lebron began, a Vietnam vet with a huge mustache and Beatles paraphernalia plastered around his bed. Earlier that day, Lebron had threatened to kick his bunkmate, Andy, in the stomach if he didn't sleep on his side in order to stop snoring so loud. "I started a bar one time out there in Santee. My friend Bob says, 'What the heck, Lebron, you know everybody out here. Why don't you start a bar?' So I say to myself, 'What the heck—'"

"Hey you! You...you guys! You ain't nothing but a bunch a...bunch a...bunch a..." Just then Denny, one of Boston's friends from New York with a northeastern accent of his own, came by on his way to an Alcoholics Anonymous meeting.

"Who the heck is that? That your friend, Boston?"

Lebron protested with anger for being interrupted.

Boston stood to address Denny, "Yeah!? How you doing?! How you doing?! It's good to see ya! It's good to see ya!"

"Have a nice day!" Lebron interrupted, waiving his hand in the air to motion Denny away.

"You…ain't no good for…good for…" Denny continued to Boston.

"I swear…I swear…I'll come over and…come over and…" Boston taunted Denny.

As Denny began to walk towards the Alcoholics Anonymous meeting, Lebron yelled at him as if carrying on an entirely different conversation, "Yeah, yeah, keep walking! Keep walking!"

Just then Walter piped in. "He pulls out a gun and I'm ducking."

"Yeah, I'm ready when you are!" Boston continued taunting Denny, putting his arms up with clenched fists as if he were Mike Tyson.

"Yeah, your momma!" Lebron yelled at Denny, getting more excited as he took his insults to the next level.

"Y'all, y'all ain't nothing but a…but a…but a…a bunch of…!" Then Denny yelled a word that made Lebron drop his cigarette. Lebron stood up.

"Ok," Lebron growled. "That's enough!" he roared. "Why don't you come here and say that to my face?!"

Just then Manny, the house manager, threw open the door to The Good Samaritan Mission. His room was right next to the entrance. "Alright, alright, knock it off you guys," he ordered to the group of us sitting on the porch.

After a minute or two things simmered down. Lebron picked up his cigarette. He sat in his plastic chair.

"What was with that guy?" asked Lyrel, referring to Denny. Lyrel, in his early twenties and heavy set, wore glasses, a solid black shirt, jean shorts, and old tennis shoes.

"He's mad at you," Boston kidded Lyrel. "I think it's your hair. He came up earlier and asked for Lyrel. Something about you wouldn't share your supper with him? Some type of supper?"

"Sure," Lyrel smirked nervously, unsure if Boston was bluffing.

"Don't believe a thing he says, Lyrel," Walter interjected. "Boston likes messing with the new people." Then Walter announced he needed to go buy some smokes. He got out of his seat and walked away.

"Wait a minute," Boston announced to the group, "Hey listen, listen, you think you can't believe anything I say, listen to this! Franken Berry—" Boston pointed to Walter who walked away, "told Daniel that he lived in CHI-NA!" Boston said China with a heavy emphasis on each syllable.

"Franken Berry lived in China?" Lebron questioned.

"Yeah!" Boston went on, "and he speaks fluent CHI-NESE and he's the king of CHI-NA!" Walter had a reputation around the Mission for exaggerating his past life experiences. I never felt any reason to believe Walter actually went to China.

Daniel, who had been sitting quietly until this point, added, "He said he studied Kung Fu."

"Listen, listen, his Kung Fu training consists of three episodes of Hong Kong Phooey!" Boston roared.

"Why do you call him Franken Berry?" Lyrel wanted to know.

"Just look at him!" The explanation was self-evident, apparently. Google revealed that Franken Berry was the mascot for a General Mills cereal. Boston was right, Walter did share a striking resemblance.

"I lived in China for a while," Daniel said.

"Really?" Lyrel asked. "What were you doing in China, Daniel?"

"Well," Daniel began, "I was vice president of the largest group of English speaking schools in China, but I was really writing a book called *No Pandas in China*. It was going to be called *Six Years in China*, but then Brad Pitt did that *Seven Years in Tibet* movie so I couldn't do that anymore, so I ended up doing twelve years in China and calling it *No Pandas in China*. But the last four years I was there I didn't have a visa. So when my apartment burned down, I lost everything, got caught without my visa, and they put me in prison for forty days before deporting me. My wife's still in China. But my book made it to Washington D.C." Daniel showed me e-mail correspondence and pictures of his wife in China and sent me a few chapters of his book, which was highly entertaining. I always believed he lived and worked in China, though I had no way to verify his work history there. At one point, Daniel actually hatched a plan to assume the identity of one of the other men at the Mission, sneak back into China, and rescue his wife. Perhaps fortunately for both of them, they never executed it.

"Huh. So who's going to publish your book?" Lebron asked.

"I hope Murdoch. They did the Johnny Cash biography, and a few other—"

"So what do you guys think about tattoos?" Lyrel interrupted.

"Huh?" Daniel responded. "That was an interesting change in conversation, Lyrel."

"I've got four," Lyrel continued. "Here!" Lyrel rolled up his black shirt sleeve. "It's a diamond. It says 'Gone, but never forgotten,' and these are my grandmother's initials, see, 'E. L. S.'"

"That's beautiful, Lyrel," Daniel said, sympathetically.

"Wait. Show me," Boston said.

"See? 'E. L. S.'" Lyrel shifted his body so Boston could see his bicep, pointing with his finger to each initial. "And I wrote a book, too," Lyrel added. "*Canopy Maneuver*. It's a sci-fi." I believed this was a fabrication.

"Oh yeah? What's it about?" Boston asked.

Lyrel lowered his voice to create suspense. "It's about this boy that gets sucked into his computer and lives in another world."

"Oh, yeah? Can I get it at the library?" Boston wanted to know.

"I don't know. Probably. *Canopy Maneuver* by Lyrel Smith. It's spelled L-Y-R-E-L, Lyrel."

"That's great, Lyrel," Daniel said. "You know, the library down here is fantastic. They've got everything."

"So do they have the *Necronomicon* there?" Lyrel wanted to know.

"What is that?" asked Daniel.

"It's the Goth Bible." Google confirmed this was roughly the case. "It's everything anti-conformist," Lyrel answered as if he were an authority on the subject and everybody else should be, too.

"What does that mean, anti-conformist?" Daniel asked.

"It's anything not normal to society," Lyrel said with even more authority to show how put out he was. "Normalness annoys me."

"Well, you're in the right place to get away from that!" Boston roared.

"You've got that right!" Daniel exclaimed, laughing as he slapped the top of his leg.

"STICK A-ROUND!" Boston's face began to turn red from laughter. "You won't have to worry about normal around here!"

Just then Walter returned. "What? Here, at The Good Samaritan Mission? No, there's not much normal here," Walter concluded, walking back into the Mission.

I got out of my seat and followed him in.

Frank stood at a table in the common area making lunch. I walked down the hall and chatted with Gerald as he did his laundry. In the back, Mattie tried to sleep while Max played the mandolin on the bunk beneath mine. Meanwhile, Lebron and his bunkmate, Andy, were nearly yelling over which of them snored louder.

———

On nights like this I wanted to speed the seven miles to my old neighborhood and honk the horn outside my friends' dads' houses, load up the truck, and bring them back to the Mission. It's not only nice to have friends, but the absence of them is a health concern. The former Surgeon General, Vivek Murthy, has said that the most common health issue in The United States is isolation, especially among men. Research suggests isolation is linked to heart disease and a shorter life span. It even registers in the brain as physical pain. As a child, I had accepted what my society subtly taught me, that I, too, must grow to become an economic engine without friends. I, too, must be a success. Living at the Mission, I unlearned this.

One day the pastor called me in his office. He sat behind his big desk while I rested in a red, comfy chair. We small chatted for a few minutes before he said, "Derek, the reason I called you in here is because I felt like I needed to share something with you, something I felt like God wanted me to give you." The pastor pulled out his Bible and flipped through the pages. He pointed at one and said, "Here, here's the verse." Then he read it out loud. "Greater love has no one than this, than to lay down one's life for his friends."

I didn't need to think before saying, "You know, pastor, I think you're right. That verse is for me." I couldn't help but want to lay down my life and love each of my friends in their own special way. And what's more, I couldn't wait for what might happen that night while they talked and smoked cigarettes.

Chapter Seven Questions:

1. Having others whom you love and support and who love and support you, headed in the same direction, is critical to living a life of purpose. Who is part of your community? Who are you supporting?

2. What intentional steps might you take to replicate every-day community like the men had at The Good Samaritan Mission?

Chapter Eight

Marion Square

Every morning Manny would hit the lights and yell, "Gentlemen! It's time to get up!" Guys would grunt and stir; lockers would bang. Manny's morning announcement reminded me a lot of my mother's when I was growing up, only she would sing at the top of her lungs, "Rise and shine! Wake up, sleepy head! Go on, it's time to get out of that bed!"

I'd ignore Manny's announcement the way I used to ignore my mother's.

"Derek, you need to get up," Manny said, shaking my arm.

I'd get up around 7:10 a.m. and have twenty minutes to shower, throw on some clothes, brush my teeth, and grab a stale bagel on my way out the door by the Mission's required 7:30 a.m. exit time.

The first couple of mornings, I left the Mission and walked down Meeting Street with a little knapsack to Marion Square, a public park in downtown Charleston, and lie on the grass. I'd think about why I was at The Good

Samaritan Mission and what I was supposed to do with my life. I'd put my knapsack down, usually with a book or two and a journal in it. Sometimes I would take out my journal and write desperate prayers and thoughts about what I saw and felt at The Good Samaritan Mission. Most of the time, I'd put the knapsack under my head and go back to sleep.

I can imagine there are plenty of people who might think, "Who has time and resources to put his life into a holding pattern in pursuit of purpose? To lounge around in a public park all day?" They might answer, "Someone who doesn't have very many responsibilities, that's who. Someone for whom keeping those dependent on him clothed and fed aren't pressing concerns." I can see them now, with their crossed arms. "Grow up out of your Peter Pan lifestyle!" their angry e-mails conclude.

And to those folks I would say, "I agree with you."

I was twenty-two years old. I had a lot of flexibility. I had little responsibility.

But I had made two decisions about my life.

One was to work incredibly hard to create seasons where I had the mental and financial space to pursue purpose. I had spent the six months before I left for Kenya, one year earlier, working like a dog as a tour guide to pay off 17,000 dollars of student loans and save up 8,000 dollars or so.

The other decision I made was to live incredibly frugally. Because I slept on a friend's couch for 350 dollars a month before Kenya, and the Mission cost 80 dollars a week, utilities and dinner included, my budget was about 1,200 dollars a month in both circumstances. I knew that if I worked three days a week as a tour guide I could save, after taxes, about 8,000 a year. I would immediately have three days a week to pursue other projects (including Saturdays). And, if I invested that savings every year between age twenty-two and sixty-five, at 10 percent, I would retire with just under 5,000,000 dollars.

I was never going to impress anyone with my nice apartment or fancy car. I eventually passed up a master's degree at New York University that would have cost 70,000 dollars. But I saw debt and society's standards as choices, not assumptions, that could restrict the financial space and time to pursue purpose. By making choices not to fit in with my peers I felt pain and self-doubt. But those choices would ultimately be the most responsible and freeing choices I could make.

One morning, not long after moving into the Mission, I began dozing off in Marion Square and was awakened by a loud voice.

"Hey, you! Get up and out of here!"

I was confused because the voice didn't sound like Manny's or my mother's. "Get up! Get up!"

Rubbing my eyes, I saw a man in a black uniform coming toward me with light glaring off his sunglasses.

"Get up!" He extended his arms forward and yelled, "You want to go downtown!?"

I did not know this man. Aren't we downtown already, I thought?

As indicated by his handcuff motions, "downtown" meant prison.

"I'm sorry. I didn't realize I couldn't sleep here," I said.

"You're — right you can't sleep here. No loitering. If I catch you here again I'm going to arrest you."

"I'm really sorry, officer," I apologized. "Just out of curiosity, why can't you sleep in Marion Square?"

I had seen people sleep at Marion Square: college girls in bikinis or bike taxi operators taking an afternoon nap.

The question must have made the officer realize I wasn't the typical 8 a.m. park sleeper. He looked at my yellow shorts, green polo shirt, and fluffy, wavy carrot-top hair.

He lowered his tone and softened his demeanor.

"You're not allowed to be in the park this early sleeping," he said as if we were close friends. "Don't worry about it. It's not a big deal. Just don't do it again before 10 a.m. or so."

"I understand," I said. I left. I couldn't sleep in the park that early because it meant I might have spent the night there, and spending the night there meant I was homeless.

I walked across Meeting Street, down Charlotte Street, and took a right on Elizabeth Street. I felt shock at being accosted for taking a nap in a public park because a police officer thought I was homeless. I held my knapsack a little tighter. I wondered, where are the homeless supposed to go? Was it right to tell people who didn't have a space of their own, of all people, that they couldn't be in a public space?

The library was only a few blocks away. When I arrived, there were thirty people or so, most of who were poorly dressed and appeared as if they already knew not to be in Marion Square at this hour. They waited for the library to open at 9 a.m. They hustled in for access to the Internet on a limited number of computers. Some picked up books, looked for somewhere to go to sleep, or simply sat, grateful to be out of the heat. I walked into the bathroom upstairs to find both sinks occupied by men who gave themselves birdbaths.

———

Later that week I wrote in my journal:

"Gandhi believed, 'No reform is possible unless some of the educated and the rich voluntarily accept the status of the poor...refuse to enjoy the amenities denied to the poor, and, instead of taking avoidable hardships, discourtesies and injustice as a matter of course, fight for their removal.'[8] It seems then that helping others requires casting off success.

Helping others also requires empathy.

The officer's misperception forces me to face the difficulty of walking in somebody else's shoes to understand their problems. It confirms that empathy doesn't happen from a distance, by donating a tidy sum at the end of the year or after seeing the picture of a hungry child on a television screen. Empathy is inherently incarnational. Empathy walks in someone else's shoes. Empathy is *voluntarily abandoning our strength for the weakness of others.* Empathy matters because before I can solve somebody else's problem I have to fully understand it myself."

Chapter Eight questions:

1. "Empathy is voluntarily abandoning our strength for the weakness of others." Understanding where someone is coming from is critical to knowing how to help them. This is true whether it is your spouse, child, coworker, neighbor, homeless person or politician. What additional steps can you take to empathize with those you would like to help?

2. I later became friends with the same officer who yelled at me in Marion Square. We frequented the same coffee shop. I never mentioned our previous encounter to him. It helped me realize how much context and environment, and our ability to understand another's context and environment, affects how we behave and treat each other. What do you think about this?

Chapter Nine
Borrowing from Dollar Bill

"Man, I've blown through millions of dollars selling cocaine," Dollar Bill said, sitting on the front porch. On his bicep was a tattoo of our first president's face on—you guessed it—a Dollar Bill.

Dollar Bill moved into The Good Samaritan Mission directly from prison. His daughter lived at the homeless shelter down the street. She came around the Mission wearing tie dye shirts with jeans and a bandana. She and her father ate at Church's Chicken together. Sometimes they went to the movies.

Dollar Bill was white, short, and had a big chest from doing a lot of pushups while behind bars. He was missing a few teeth and shaved his head, never missing a hair. "Man, there was only one time I really thought I was going to have to kill a guy," he continued. "We were in a hotel room and he just burst in wearing a mask, almost as if it was by — accident. He shot at me and I shot back. We both missed. Then he ran, got in his car, and sped away. I had a couple hundred thousand dollars on me in cash and cocaine.

"But that was a different life," he said, exhaling before concluding. "Man, I must have blown through millions of dollars selling cocaine," he repeated, still shaking his head. Dollar Bill tapped his finger on the end of his cigarette. "You know, sometimes I wish somebody would have shown me how to save growing up. In my previous profession, I made money so quickly that I got used to spending it just as quick, and living like that for so long makes it hard to change."

Dollar Bill, more than any of the other men from the Mission, liked to come to church. He said, "I need all the church I can get." The first Sunday he came he wanted to attend the newcomer's class.

At the class a staff member from the church thanked us for coming and asked what we thought about the message. "I thought it was real good," Dollar Bill said. "Real authentic," he added. We sat at a table with my bunkmate from The Good Samaritan Mission, Frank, and a family with their thirteen-year-old son. The mother had fluffy blonde hair with bright streaks, a tint of red in her lips, and broad shoulders. Her husband sat to her right wearing a polo shirt and sunglasses with a body that used its annual gym membership. The staff member asked us to go around the table and tell everyone what brought us to church today. The family told us they were new to town and were looking for a church home.

When it came to Dollar Bill's turn, he looked at the wife and with his fingertips tapping together and a serious look on his face asked, "Do you believe in the power of prayer?" Until then the wife obliged Dollar Bill's small talk but seemed more interested in the church brochures in front of her. The wife tilted her head as if to say Dollar Bill's question was not only rhetorical but borderline childish and entirely too personal. But Dollar Bill held his ground, without blinking.

"Yes, of course I believe in the power of prayer," she said.

"Okay then," Dollar Bill said, now pushing his head a little lower and forward across the table, raising his pupils to where they met his eye lids, "Let me tell you a little something about myself."

Dollar Bill began his story in 2002, when he first moved to Charleston from Ohio. In 2003 his son was born, in 2004 he and his wife became separated, at which point he admits a turn for the worse. By the end of 2004 he was both a cocaine dealer and addict and was incarcerated in the summer of 2006. I thought the husband and wife and teenage son's eyeballs might pop out if they stared any harder. Dollar Bill concluded with, "I just got out of prison on Monday for serving three years for dealing cocaine. I'm trying to keep clean, and I thought church would be a good place to do that. That's why I'm here. I'm here because I believe in the power of prayer."

I wondered what would happen next, if the family might leave or call security. I worried I wouldn't be allowed back to church. That's when the father looked at Dollar Bill and said, "My sixteen-year-old son is a cocaine addict."

"Dad!" the younger son said, "maybe he can help Ryan!"

Dollar Bill told the family about how he needed a job, how one of his daughters was in foster care, and how he needed prayer. "God was with me in prison. At one point I hadn't heard from a soul in three months, not my wife, not my children, not the lawyer I'd been paying. I was in my cell alone on my knees begging and crying to God to give me anything, anything at all, any hope. That's when the intercom asked for 'William Hollis.' The guard came to get me and led me into the visiting area where I saw my lawyer's secretary. It was just my lawyer's secretary, but it was also God, telling me that he hadn't left me, that he was still there, that there was a reason to have hope. There's hope for your son," Dollar Bill said.

By the time the family had finished telling Dollar Bill about their sixteen-year-old son, the newcomer's meeting was over. The family and Dollar Bill swapped information, and the father even said he would help Dollar Bill find a job.

As we drove home across the bridge in my truck, with Frank in the middle and Dollar Bill on the passenger side, Dollar Bill looked at me and said, "Derek, I really enjoyed that. Thank you for taking me." Then he added the thing he would always say, "I just pray that God will do for me what I can't do for myself."

———

Dollar Bill, like many of the men I met who were released from prison, was an entrepreneur. In Dollar Bill's case, he found it hard to work for others after having worked for himself.

Dollar Bill came home one day with dirt on his head.

"What did you do at work today?" I asked.

"Man, I slept," he said.

"You slept?"

"Yeah, man. I crawled under a building at the construction site and slept. It's too hot to be working for seven dollars and twenty-five cents an hour. I ain't working in the heat for that."

Even while Dollar Bill slept on the job he managed to start a side business collecting scrap metal and copper from job sites to sell on the weekends.

"Hey, Derek," he said one Friday night, "I got a business proposition for you." He exuded the confidence of an executive for a Fortune 500 company. But then Dollar Bill moved too close. His chest got a little bigger, and I felt like I was trying to avoid a kiss on our first date.

"Oh yeah?" I said, taking a step back.

"Yeah, if you'll take me to the scrap yard tomorrow, I'll do your weekend chore," he said, referring to each resident's responsibility to do a chore around the Mission. He stepped another inch closer.

I thought for a brief second before saying, "No, thanks. I'm not interested."

Dollar Bill took a step back. He looked at me cross. "Fine then," he blurted, "why you got to be like that? Why should I even bother telling you my ideas?"

While I didn't appreciate his attitude, I agreed Dollar Bill could pay me a few dollars for gas, and I would be willing to give him a ride.

The next morning, we drove the relatively abandoned and industrial spine of the city, headed towards the scrap yard with Dollar Bill's metal in the back of my truck. We were small chatting when Dollar Bill said it again, "I just pray that God will do for me what I can't do for myself." I nearly asked what he meant by that before assuming it was the same for Dollar Bill as it was the rest of us: a family, a good paying job, to be "successful"—the American Dream.

By the time I'd parked my truck, Dollar Bill was already unpacking suitcases full of copper wire onto a giant scale. He had some "copper one" and "copper two." They were different prices by the pound. The copper one was thinner and lighter in color. The copper two was thicker and darker. I helped Dollar Bill unload the suitcases and then continued eating my banana.

The scrap yards were in a different part of town, one of those parts of town I'd seen only when passing from the interstate in the roughly twenty years of living in Charleston. The scrap yard was a couple of bare buildings with a big scale for trucks to pull onto and a few smaller scales for things you load yourself. There were piles of metal and copper and steel everywhere. I watched as Dollar Bill finished loading everything on the scale and tossed my banana peel in the trash can.

On the drive home, Dollar Bill told me what he planned to do with the one hundred and twenty dollars he got for selling copper. "You know man, I'm taking my sister Sally out tonight. I haven't seen her since I went to prison, and she's getting out right now." She'd been incarcerated sometime after Dollar Bill had, and when he'd gotten out she was still in. "You know," Dollar Bill said, "Sally has ruined a lot of people's lives, partially including mine. She's spent tens of thousands of dollars of my cocaine merchandise, you know, but —," he continued, "she's still my sister." We took a right and began to cross a bridge over a railroad. A few abandoned railroad cars sat off to one side. "When I was in jail I didn't know if she was dead or alive. I knew that she was out there on the streets hanging with the wrong crowd, and I just prayed that she was alive, and you know, God doesn't usually answer my prayers the way I want him to, but he answers them the way he knows is best. So when I got out and found she was in, I knew she was still alive."

As I listened to Dollar Bill, I thought about the night we first met, only a few days after he got out of prison. He was excited, holding a giant, black garbage bag in his hands. "Man, I just met up with the guy who ratted me out to the cops," he said. "When I was in jail the guy just kept contacting my ex-wife over and over again, telling her how sorry he was for what he did to me. The guy really wished he hadn't ratted me out. I think he was nervous I'd either kill him or have somebody else kill him." Dollar Bill raised the huge trash bag. "He just gave me all these clothes!"

I couldn't understand how, in Dollar Bill's eyes, everything that had happened between him and the person who ratted him out was just water under the bridge. "I don't know man," Dollar Bill told me, "I just figure the more you hold on to something, the more it's got a hold on you."

"It's like this about my sister Sally," Dollar Bill said on our drive back to the Mission. "Christ tells us that we have to forgive others if we want to be forgiven." Then he tapped me on the shoulder. I glanced over to the passenger seat and made eye contact. "Ain't that right?"

———

Later that evening I wrote in my journal:

"Christ tells us to forgive others so that we, too, may be forgiven. Living at the Mission is showing me how much of my behavior and outlook towards society disregards his command. As a college graduate with a middle class pathway laid out for me, the American Dream consistently tells me I'm a success. I spend most of my time with those who are pretty much like me. I behave pretty much the same way as everybody else, focused on minor adjustments like recycling and buying fair trade coffee. We collectively reinforce to each other that we're doing right, and the areas where we're wrong can't be that wrong because, after all, everybody we know is doing it. We perceive ourselves as needing little forgiveness and consequently extend it quite sparingly.

On the other hand, Dollar Bill's criminal record and drug history make him a reject by society's standards, drastically limiting his options for employment, housing, education, the ability to vote, and more. He and others like him live on the streets and under bridges and in shelters and prisons and ghettos. These failures by American culture's standards have no illusions about their need for forgiveness, and consequently receive and extend it far more freely than I.

Failing systematically, structurally, and indirectly to forgive seems to reinforce living fragmented and segregated from those who are different from us. This hurts us in a couple of ways.

One, it builds mistrust, fear, resentfulness, and an unwillingness to work together among individuals and groups.

Two, we're blinded from our flaws and opportunities to grow when we live separate from those who behave and think differently from us. In my case, I have to unlearn much of what I thought about both Dollar Bill and myself in order to learn about forgiveness.

Lastly, we risk living very narrow lives that cannot empathize with, serve, help others, and in turn gain purpose. We risk losing our opportunity to meet Christ, who insists that when we see his face we'll realize we've really known it all along from the faces of others. He'll tell us that when he was hungry we either did or didn't give him something to eat, when he was thirsty we either did or didn't give him something to drink, when he was a stranger we either did or didn't invite him in, when he needed clothes we either did or didn't clothe him, when he was sick we either did or didn't care for him, and when he was in prison we either did or didn't visit him. When we ask when we did or did not do these things, he'll say it was all indirectly. 'Whatever you did for one of the least of these brothers of mine, you did for me.'[9]

I can miss Jesus simply by choosing to live according to society's unwritten and unquestioned rules that keep people Jesus says are himself from coming around. Why do I keep Jesus away? Is it because he's a criminal? But if I want to be close to him wouldn't I also want a prison in my neighborhood so I could visit him more conveniently? Is it because he's uneducated? But which is better, learning a degree for a job or forgiveness for the soul? Or is it because he's poor and needy? But wouldn't I give up a higher real estate value to be able to live closer to Jesus? Danish politician Ditlev Gothard Monrad observed 'that the human heart houses cravings to which it gives false names in order to justify love for them...greed is called concern for spouse and children.'[10] At least Dollar Bill is honest enough to tattoo his love on his arm."

———

A few weeks later Dollar Bill disappeared from the Mission. I didn't know where he was for months until my bunkmate Frank came home and reported he'd seen him that day.

Frank worked through a labor agency sanding cement blocks. They were building a new prison and every block in the place had to be sanded. Frank saw this as "job security." The new prison was next to the old prison. Frank was sanding blocks on the third floor of the new prison when he looked down in the old prison's yard and saw a familiar bald head in an orange jumpsuit with a Dollar Bill tattoo on his bicep.

It took me several weeks to see him. First I had to write. Then he had to schedule me an appointment, which I didn't know about until it was too late. When I finally walked down a long, white hall to see him on the other side of a video screen, he told me the same thing again, that "on the outside I just kept asking God to do for me what I couldn't do for myself." It seemed to me, then, that God must have failed Dollar Bill.

"Man, Derek, I'm only in here on a brushed up charge for possession of marijuana, but man, I've been doing cocaine daily for months behind everybody's back. I was carrying around a sample of my daughter's urine in case the pastor drug tested me." I looked at the top of his bald head with a telephone pressed to his ear and his elbow sticking straight up in the air somewhere in Leeds Prison, laughing at his delayed jokes as they came through the receiver.

Dollar Bill finished his story with, "But I just kept asking God to do for me what I couldn't do for myself." He said this shaking his head, as if in awe and disbelief, as if he had expected one thing and gotten another.

When he began to tell me how he'd buried himself in his Bible, how he had grown close to God, how he was going to write the pastor a letter, and how next time when he got out it would be different, I began to tune him out. I'd heard these sorts of things before, how someone was sorry, how they had changed. Dollar Bill went on for five minutes telling me these things until finally, after a deep breath, he finished with, "...and then God did."

The deep breath broke my daze. I looked up and asked, "God did what?"

"He forgave me and got me off the drugs," Dollar Bill said. "God did for me what I couldn't do for myself."

Chapter Nine Questions:

1. How might forgiveness on a more systemic level play out and affect our broader society?

2. "I can miss Jesus simply by choosing to live according to society's unwritten and unquestioned rules that keep people Jesus says are Himself from coming around." What do you think about this? Do you think you keep Jesus away? Why or why not?

3. Have you ever been put into "prison" for your own good to remove you from a situation in which you were exhibiting bad behavior?

Chapter Ten

Carriage Tours

I moved into The Good Samaritan Mission on June 1, 2009. By the middle of July, I started working as a carriage driver again, the same job through which I'd paid off my student loans the prior year.

"Carriage tours" in Charleston refers to the largest horse-and-mule-drawn carriage industry in the world. I gave one-hour tours to as many as eight groups of sixteen people on a daily basis, guiding a team of horses or mules through the historic streets of Charleston in the blazing summer heat. While most tour guides were a wellspring of knowledge, to be honest, I stuck mostly to my own worn-out script.

By the sixth tour of the day, I'd forget if I was repeating my short circuit of facts and stories to the same group. I'd look up at four rows of four people each, mostly moms and dads with kids and hats and water bottles and sunscreen. Everybody was sweating and had a glazed-over look. I'd ask, "Have I already told you guys about the palmetto tree?"

"This would be the third time," somebody said.

"Right. We won't do that again then," I said. "Is

everybody having a great time?" I didn't want to lose my job.

In downtown Charleston there was a very small group of old residents who did not appreciate slow-moving, tourist-bearing, traffic-creating carriages on their streets. Sometimes they got right on my rear bumper to let me know to speed up. Other times they sped around me to let me know I was in the way. One particular time, just to show some Southern hospitality, one kind soul rolled down the window and yelled at me:

"You're driving too slow! Pull over!"

The residents typically drove Volvos and BMWs. The carriage was much higher from the ground. I crouched down to see a big pearl necklace, huge earrings, colored hair, and flushed cheeks leaning across into the passenger's seat and jabbing a finger at me. I listened and took it all in.

"I'm so sorry ma'am," I said, "I'm doing my very best, and I'll do better next time." I smiled really big. When she sped off, I looked back at the tour group. They looked like we were all in kindergarten, and I had been yelled at by the teacher. Then I joked, "That was my mom!" All the tourists laughed.

It's often easy to look back fondly on something that at the time didn't seem that great. I loved the carriage company, the industry, the tourists, the animals, my coworkers and managers—but I knew it wasn't my final destination.

Between every tour I ran to the bathroom, got on my knees with the door locked, and prayed, "Dear God, I made a promise that if you gave me something meaningful to do I wouldn't quit until you said it was time to quit or until it was complete. Now I'm living in a homeless shelter and I don't know why. Where is the meaningful thing to do?" I was tired of waiting. I thought about moving out and living a normal life and getting a job like the ones my papa told me about when I was young. By the time I got back from the bathroom, less than five minutes later, another tour group was ready to go.

I wished somebody could have talked to me while I was on my hands and knees in that bathroom, praying for something better to do.

"Everything will be okay," I wish they'd said. "You're going to have ups and downs and every day you will feel like there is an important vision you want to see brought to fruition. God will fulfill his purpose for you because of his great unfailing love, for you and for the world. But please stop your complaining."

My ears would have perked up.

"The speaking skills you're learning by giving tours will serve you well in the future. You are making friends you will love for years to come. This pit stop has meaning. You are growing in important things like gratitude and patience and perseverance. Believe it or not," they might finish with, "while you're on your hands and knees now, acting a little pathetic, you'll look back on this time with a lot of joy."

———

One day after work I was shooting the breeze with my boss, Barry, when he asked me where I was living. Barry was a big guy, six feet four inches tall and sturdy. He was leaning back in his chair with his hands behind his head.

"The Good Samaritan Mission," I said.

"What is that?" he asked. I told him. He put his hands down on his armchair and raised his eyebrows. His eyes got big. "What the heck, Snook? Do you need to stay with me?"

"No, it isn't like that," I said.

"Then what's it like?" He asked.

"It's like, well, I just feel like I'm supposed to live there. If Jesus came to earth to walk in our shoes and, in part, to solve our problems, it seems like we should do the same for others even in comparably insignificant ways," I said. "I guess I've been thinking that by living there I might figure out how to better help."

"Holy crap!" Barry said as if he'd seen a unicorn in the window behind me. "Snook, I don't know if I even believe in God, but you're a saint. You want to grab a beer?"

I wasn't a saint, but Barry's comment showed how my willingness to live with the homeless gave me credibility that just talking about the homeless didn't. I wasn't talking at my boss about what mattered most to me. I was showing my boss.

I grabbed my knapsack and carriage whip and walked up Anson Street in the shade of the buildings and trees, all the way across Calhoun Street, jig-sawing my way to Nassau Street (where supposedly Chip killed his friend Listerine Sam). I walked in the front door of the Mission and looked at the board with all of our pictures to see if anybody had arrived or left that day. After small chatting with the guys huddled around the T.V. watching the news, I grabbed my towel from my bunk bed, took a shower, and had dinner with the twenty-some other men at the Mission.

After dinner, men sat around the front porch while they smoked. I sat and listened, watching the sun set behind the *Post and Courier*'s building. I had to run to the Family Dollar and made it back just before eleven when Manny locked the doors. Everybody else was in bed when I brushed my teeth next to my bunkmate, Frank, and set my alarm for the next morning. Some of the men snored. A locker door or two clanged open and shut. Somebody passed gas.

I climbed the small ladder to my top bunk and crouched into the fetal position to say a few quick prayers. As I took a deep breath, I felt a tingling start in my head and spread through my entire body.

I couldn't stop Thoreau's thoughts from rushing to my mind, that most men live lives of quiet desperation; but if you pursue the life you've dreamed of you'll find a different kind of success in the most common of hours.[11] Laying in my bunk bed with twenty-five other men who couldn't even afford places of their own, I realized I was exactly where I was supposed to be, doing what I was supposed to do. I realized there is no such thing as success or failure, only *purpose*.

Chapter Ten Questions:

1. It was difficult for me to be in the waiting room of doing carriage tours while my purpose unfolded. I nearly gave up. What waiting room are you in? What can you learn there while you wait?

2. What do you think about the concept of talking at someone versus showing someone what is important to you? Have you ever tried to change people by telling them things? Do you ever see this practiced in broader society? How instead might you show them?

Chapter Eleven

Working Day Labor

My near-arrest experience at Marion Square showed me that at some level I could empathize with the men at The Good Samaritan Mission. I could, in some small way, understand their problems. Now, I wanted to find a way to help.

I lived where they lived, slept where they slept, ate where they ate, and I wondered what else I could do.

Before I lived at The Good Samaritan Mission I assumed all homeless people were unemployed. It surprised me that many worked full time. I felt people who worked forty hours a week or more should be able to afford a home. I wanted to understand how they could still be homeless. Having noticed most of the guys worked at a day labor agency a few blocks away, I decided I wanted to work where they worked. That meant quitting my job at the carriage company.

There were a few reasons I didn't want to quit my job. For one, I'd be making one-third of my earnings at the carriage company, since day labor paid minimum wage at seven dollars and twenty-five cents an hour (minimum wage in the state of South Carolina has not risen since I worked day labor in 2009). For another, I was somewhat scared of the manual labor. My mom gave me a few more reasons when I called from my flip-phone. I caught her at a bad time. When I told her, "Mom, I'm going to quit my job and work day labor," it was too much for her motherly soul to bear.

"No!" she pleaded into the phone. "Derek, you'll be wasting the talents God gave you if you do that." I hated to lose her approval.

I waited a few days and called her back. "If you think it's what you need to do, then you should do it," she responded, to my surprise.

The day I quit, Ben, one of my managers, said, "I could tell something was on your mind, Snook." I loved the folks at the carriage company, but working day labor could help me better understand why the guys at the Mission were stuck. When I told Ben what I wanted to do he told me he understood. "If you got an itch, you got to scratch it, Snook," he said in the manner of a wise philosopher.

Barry said, "Snook, you're crazy." I caught him after he had a few beers at Big Frank's. Barry shortened my two weeks' notice and told me if I wanted to come back I could.

———

I began working day labor in the middle of August of 2009.

While jobs typically didn't start until 7 a.m., you needed to show up at the labor agency by 5:30 a.m. if you hoped to get on a ticket. The first morning, I was up by 4:45 a.m. Raul, one of the guys from the Mission, assured me he could get me a job. I wore my college fraternity shirt. I also had on some brand new, tan, Timberland steel-toed boots from Walmart.

"It will be easy to get you on a ticket," Raul said. "You've got a truck so you can take other guys to work with you." When we showed up, I saw fifty to sixty guys outside, some with vehicles and most without, in a partial grass, gravel, and cracked-concrete parking lot. Most guys drank their morning coffee or beer, and everybody smoked their morning cigarette.

Raul took me around the side of the building, vomit orange in color, down a narrow alley to the entrance. The building used to be an auto repair shop, and when the business changed, the old garage became the new waiting room. Another twenty-five to thirty guys were inside, most sitting in chairs, and a few people were passed out in the corners on the floor. A line formed in front of a small glass window. When Raul and I got to the front, he signed his name to the list and told me to do the same.

"Jeff!" Raul yelled through the glass and began knocking on the window. "Hey, Jeff!" Raul continued to yell and knock. Jeff popped from around the corner. He was in his thirties and wore a collared shirt. "This is Derek," Raul continued. "He's got a truck. You think you can get him out on a ticket?" Jeff handed me a short application form and an I-9 and W-4, which I filled out.

We went back outside and around the building. I sat down with my back against the wall. I pulled my Bible out of my small knapsack. I looked across King Street at the courtyard of a Catholic school. The sun poked over the school and glared in my eyes. Periodically, Jeff would come out and scan the faces in the crowd. The men would say, "Jeff! Jeff! You got something for me?"

He'd ignore them and keep scanning, walking in and out of the building, occasionally handing tickets to different employees. A few minutes after 6 a.m. he came up to Raul. We held our breath. He gave Raul a ticket. Raul turned to me and said, "Ready to go, compadre?"

Five of us—two in the cab and three in the bed—drove in my truck out to a hospital under construction about half an hour outside of town. Each employee had to pay two dollars and fifty cents each way to the driver. We showed up a few minutes before 7 a.m. and reported to an electrical company. After a one-hour safety course and a ten-minute exam, they put me on the job for my first assignment of day labor.

Our task for the day wasn't the worst—we could have been digging ditches in the sweltering heat. Nor was it the best—like pushing a broom and cleaning up. Our job was to "pull wire."

These weren't small wires. It took eight grown men to pull them. Our job was to pull the wire to a foreman who would guide it into a hole. The wire was attached to a system that would direct it underneath the ground to a larger electrical room, detached from the rest of the hospital. The electrical room was a couple hundred yards away. Between pulls, they'd have us unload wire from a truck and clean up.

Employees from the electrical company and other companies would say things like, "Oh, you're just a temp."

If they didn't like how we did something they would say, "If you can't do this, tomorrow I'll get somebody else from the temp agency."

When our supervisor wasn't around, an employee from another company came up and said, "Hey, y'all come over here and clean up this room. Here, clean here. Move all of this stuff over there." We helped sweep the room and took materials to a dumpster. We were being ordered to do work that wasn't our responsibility.

Larry from New Jersey kept saying to the rest of us, "They told me they were going to hire me on, permanently!"

Guys said contractors would say they were hiring whether they really were or not. This would help get a few good days' work out of us. Even so, I felt a tinge of jealousy. Why wouldn't they hire me permanently?

When it was time for a pull we would all gather around the hall outside of a small electrical room. We'd set the wires up on the pulleys in their proper places. There were five large rings of wires, each ring requiring two grown men to carry. Two rings would go on one bar and three rings would go on the bar behind it. All five rings pointed towards the electrical room.

José, an employee of the contractor, would stand behind the bars facing the rest of us. José would push the wires and make sure they came smoothly off of the ring. The rest of us would pull. "Pull! Pull! Pull!" we shouted. The guys and I grunted as we pulled.

Gary was in his late fifties. He was tall and lanky with black skin and gray fuzz for a beard. He spent most of the time talking about his "old lady," who he claimed made him work. We all learned about his pretty active sex life, both with his "old lady" and a few others, each of whom he described to us in detail, the pros and cons of each. He would talk about them between, and even during, pulls. It seemed like he would need the money with all those women to keep happy. That's why I was surprised he came to work only a few days a week.

When Gary didn't show, the other guys would guess which woman kept him out too late the night before. The next day, when Gary returned, the guys would say, "We were worried about you, Gary! Thought Sandra or Menthia might be keeping you out too late!" Gary's performance fed the stigma day laborers have, stereotypes like "Dial-a-Drunk."

Even so, as we pulled, I marveled at how the hospital wouldn't have electricity without our work. We had a really important job; the other guys knew it, too. It's just that since it was hard, manual work and required little skill, the best candidates were people who needed money so urgently they would accept seven dollars and twenty-five cents on an hourly basis, knowing they would walk away with cash the same day.

Between working and riding to and from the job, I learned about the other guys' lives. I got to know Devon who was in his late twenties. He told me he lived with his aunt and uncle and—though he worked day labor every day—couldn't afford a place of his own. I met one of his friends, Travon. After work, Travon had another job at Ryan's

Steakhouse. He was in the same boat, unable to earn enough for a place of his own. The same was true of guys like Frank and Raul at the Mission.

"Why even bother?" Raul asked as we drove through the affluent suburb, Mt. Pleasant, and back to The Good Samaritan Mission in the city. "Even if you get work every day at minimum wage, at forty hours you're basically making two hundred and fifty dollars a week, or a thousand dollars a month. You can't live on that." The guys who did have their own place and worked at the labor agency spent sixty percent or more of their monthly pay on rent and had just a few hundred dollars left over every month for food, transportation, clothing, laundry, utilities, and other essentials.

A few days later I was assigned to clean up duty. They gave me a broom and a dustpan. I walked around the hospital for eight hours cleaning. I felt like I'd be cleaning every day for the rest of my life.

Still, when I'd walk to the Porta-Potti, the inside of which reeked even worse during the hot summer months, I'd stop and raise my hands to the air. "Thank you, God," I would say. While I didn't understand what I was thanking God for and felt discouraged, I had faith that my decision to work day labor was in some way meaningful and the right decision. The faith part popped up every now and then like a ten-minute water break from the wire-pulling and mundane, endless cleaning. I savored every drop.

———

At the end of the second week of working day labor at the hospital, our foreman pulled me and one of the guys to a side job. We were following his instructions when the head superintendent for the electrical company came storming up.

Bobby Joe usually barged in to yell announcements like, "Hurry the heck up!" This time he began yelling at the foreman. "What the — is taking so long?!" he yelled. I couldn't hear the foreman's response, but whatever it was only made Bobby Joe madder. "That's —! I'll throw you off this job, and you know it!" I heard. Bobby Joe proceeded to throw things around, including the foreman's tools. He kicked a bucket. Then he picked up a metal bar and swung it so hard that, had it not just barely missed me, it would have knocked me out. "We're paying too much — money for these — temps not to be using them!" Bobby Joe stormed off. I scampered up after him.

After ten yards I piped up nervously: "How much are you paying for us, exactly?"

"I don't know. About fifteen dollars an hour!" he stomped down the hall as if he intended to cause an earthquake.

I stood in silence. I made seven dollars and twenty-five cents an hour. The electrical company claimed they were paying fifteen dollars an hour. I did the math in my head. The difference was seven dollars and seventy-five cents to the day labor agency per hour—more than I made for pulling wire.

Standing in the hall while the job continued around me,

I had an idea. If I invested in employees who showed up every day and worked hard like Devon and Travon—through things like better pay, support, and helping them find permanent jobs—while I weeded out employees like Gary who just wanted their money for the night and whose poor attendance hurt the customer by having to retrain constantly, then I could help employees improve their lives while creating a higher quality service for customers.

At lunch I went to my truck and called my dad. The phone rang a few times before he picked up. He was at work.

"Hey Derek," he said.

I told him what had happened.

"Huh, that's interesting," he said.

I exclaimed, "Dad! I'm going to start a day labor agency!"

"Sounds great, son," he said.

————

Each of us wants approval from whomever we are working for. I found something important to the one I wanted to please.

I made a promise in the back of a fourth grade classroom in Kenya. I told God if he gave me something meaningful to do I wouldn't quit until he said it was time to quit or it was complete.

Part of me expected the pursuit of purpose and success to work the same way. I thought starting a better day labor agency would be like taking an important assignment nobody else wanted. I'd raise my hand, do it, and get promoted to better assignments.

But the other part of me realized that purpose wasn't a mechanical formula or a resume builder like my cousins and papa suggested. Those were both stepladders to say or do to gain success. Purpose did not guarantee pleasure or the absence of pain. It didn't explain itself or listen to my coaching advice. The pursuit of purpose could be wild and uncertain. The reward for purpose was knowing the assignment—whether it was working with the homeless, those suffering from a disability, running a cash register or a hedge fund—mattered. I wanted it.

Chapter Eleven Questions:

1. The desire for or fear of losing approval is a significant reason why we get distracted from purpose. Initially my idea to work day labor was frowned upon by those close to me. Have you ever frowned upon someone else's idea that didn't initially make sense? Has anyone ever frowned on your idea? How might this distract you from your purpose or the purpose of somebody else?

2. "Each of us wants approval from whomever we are working for. I found something important to the one I wanted to please." What do you think about this statement? When you look closely at your life, how you spend your time and money and the things you say and do, where you live and work, who are you working to please?

Chapter Twelve
Understanding a Story

Taking the time to understand someone's story leads to grace.

Living with the homeless for a year taught me that when I understand why people behave the way they behave, I can see myself in them. Does that excuse bad behavior or mean that I have to agree with their decisions or beliefs? I don't think so. But it inspires love. Love tries solutions to cure society's problems. Judgment builds walls and distance that make society's problems worse.

———

The entire week before Labor Day weekend, I thought of how little money the homeless made. And how much they spent. Not all of them, but some of them. Well, okay, most of them.

Some of the homeless got checks on the first of the month and spent it all by the third. Others asked for quarters and nickels and dimes in front of convenience stores. Some bummed cigarettes all day long. Some guys made fifty dollars a day working for day labor agencies and spent it all on crack that night, and some stuck it in their pockets and saved it all. Occasionally, I heard a story about a homeless guy walking around with fifty thousand dollars in a duffel bag. Or a guy who used to be a professor before losing his wife and child in an auto accident. He walked around in his sadness, with a large gray beard and torn T-shirt and jeans, sleeping behind a dumpster. Then there were the few who made it out of homelessness by pulling themselves up by their own bootstraps.

As soon as work was over, guys walked down the street to the corner market or the grocery store and cashed their checks. Not all of them. Some of them. Then they bought a lottery ticket or a beer, and everybody—I mean everybody—got a pack of cigarettes. It sometimes felt like watching a man say, "I don't have enough water to drink," as he poured his glass out into the sink.

I asked around about a hypothetical budget, one a man could strive for and live on to make it out of homelessness. I felt a home was an inherent right for someone willing to work a full time job. But the answers were the same: homeless people don't save money; they're irresponsible.

I heard a parable about two homeless men. One kept his money in the bank while the other didn't. Instead, he kept it in a wad in a big rubber band in his pocket. The one who kept it in the bank made it out, got an apartment, and lives a peachy life with Jesus now. But the other got drunk one night and spent it on a hooker who stole his wad of cash the next morning. She took his pants too. I imagined this hooker, wild-eyed and crazy-haired, running across the motel parking lot and down the street in high heels with his pant legs flowing in the wind and him chasing her in his whitey-tighties, yelling and trying to light a cigarette.

After that, of course, the man who lost his wad of cash relapsed.

———

Judgment is a mental tool we use. When we judge we create a false sense of superiority over others. We pin people down to have answers to the questions we do not know. We want control without responsibility for the results.

Pinning people down means that if they follow my advice and it works out, it is because of me; I am the hero. If they do not do what I say and things do not work out, it isn't my fault and I am not responsible. If they actually make a better move for themselves, and it isn't done my way, I assume the worst. And if they do what I say and it still doesn't work, I can find a way to blame it on them—plant some bottles of liquor under their bed or blame it on their criminal background. "They just came from too broken of a home," I might add.

A still, small voice whispers behind the judgment. It has values beyond my understanding. It sees things with clarity that I do not. It tells my heart that a life of societal acceptance is not what matters most, for a homeless man or for myself. The still, small voice says judgment doesn't matter, yet judgment can blind me from what does.

The still, small voice offends my pride. "Don't tell me

what a homeless man needs," I rebuke the voice. "I know what a homeless man needs! He needs a home!" Accepting that a homeless man needs more than a home, or an unemployed man needs more than a job, or a man without pants needs a shirt and a cigarette, too, means it may not do any good to give him what I think he needs. It would be like bandaging the blister on a man's foot while he was having a heart attack.

———

Gerald was a fifty-something-year-old black man with one front tooth who bragged about his twenty-something-year-old body when he wore a tank top and described funny, made-up fantasies—some of which were sexual—about midgets.

Gerald and I would sometimes walk to the day labor agency from The Good Samaritan Mission together even though we were on different assignments.

The Friday night of Labor Day weekend, Gerald asked if I would take him to Walmart to buy a barbeque grill the next evening. Gerald didn't ask for favors very often, but he also asked if I would pay his cell phone bill the next morning while he was at work.

The next morning, I walked into the cell phone store just across the parking lot to pay Gerald's bill. It was more than I expected. I breathed a little easier when they said I could put down only the twenty dollars Gerald had given me. He could pay the rest later. I walked out the door and back to the Mission where I laid a receipt showing that he owed another sixty-seven dollars, more than an entire day's work, on Gerald's bed.

That same night, Gerald and I went to Walmart to buy a new grill. According to Gerald, "The grill I have is too dirty to use." As we drove, I thought about Gerald, who was homeless, needed money to live, owed sixty-seven dollars on his cell phone bill, and felt the best use of his money was to buy a new grill when he already had one. I supposed cleaning the grill was not an option.

We walked into Walmart. Charles told me once, before he got kicked out for coming in drunk and peeing on Frank's bed one night, "I used to get a shopping cart and fill it to the brim with groceries and walk around Walmart. Then I'd pick up a pack of long straws and a pack of Smirnoff Ice and sit the pack where the baby belongs." Charles walked around Walmart with his head real low to the shopping cart, concentrating on school supplies and sporting equipment, drinking from a straw behind a shopping cart filled to the brim. "Then I'd hide the empty bottles in the toy section."

As we walked through the store I thought of Boston, who said he used to make three hundred dollars a week at Walmart by taking two specific things—he didn't know exactly what they were—from the electronics section. He placed them behind some flower pots in the gardening section. Then he walked out of the store and around to the other side of the fence, pulled the things through, and came back in to return them. Boston rotated Walmarts, hitting a different one each time.

Gerald and I shopped for a few minutes before he bought

a thirty-seven-dollar grill, flirting with the cash register attendant on our way out.

On the ride home, Gerald said something that confirmed my judgment.

"Derek, I'm worried about paying my rent this week," he said.

We came to a stoplight and I turned to look at Gerald.

"Why are you worried, Gerald?" I asked.

He looked at his hands in his lap.

"I've got a court hearing on Tuesday," he said, "but I can't afford to miss a day at work and pay my rent."

What!? How could Gerald know all of that and then go buy a brand new grill?

We took a left turn onto Highway 17 and began driving under the overpass of Interstate 526. "Gerald," I said, "why would you go buy a grill"—which cost almost half of his weekly rent— "when you already owe sixty-seven dollars for your phone bill and you knew you needed to have some extra money so you could go to this hearing?" There. I'd said it. I glanced over to see Gerald's reaction. He stayed focused on his hands in his lap. Then he looked up at the road.

"I need a break from all this," he explained. He exhaled and shook his head like he was getting something off his chest. His shoulders lowered. His bottom lip stuck out a bit. Gerald stopped being the heedless spender and turned into a defenseless and innocent child. "I need a break from this place," he said, "something to help me forget that I am where I am because I don't have any other choice."

Oh. I believed people like Gerald were stupid. They had

to be. Anybody knew a grill was less important than a place to sleep. People like Gerald—from a standpoint that a home was an obvious thing you needed to function and live—were irresponsible. They got what they deserved. Gerald had brought this on himself. I washed my hands clean.

When we got back to the Mission, Gerald took his grill inside and came back and sat on the front porch with me. We looked out at the Alcoholics Anonymous building, the Sherwin William's paint store, and across Meeting Street at the *Post and Courier* building.

Gerald tried clinching his hand but couldn't close it all the way. He had a mini-stroke just a few days back and had to go to the hospital—another bill—and since then had been trying to close his hand over and over again, each time with a grimace on his face.

"We just don't have a lot to rally around in this place," Gerald told me, leaning forward and looking me in the eyes. "What do you think we have to rally around?" he asked.

"Well," I said, "we have God." I immediately felt like a nuisance of a Christian.

"You're right," Gerald said. "But most of the guys here don't believe in God, and those who do hardly rally around him. I just thought that a grill might bring us together, that's all. You know, it's something guys can do and sit around and talk."

I began to realize as much of what Gerald wasn't saying as what he was. In the past year he had become homeless, had some health issues, had fallen off his bike and had to go to the hospital, and then he had the mini-stroke. He was also diabetic. Just within the past year Gerald lost his father, and every so often it would be obvious something was wrong—when Gerald shared it was the anniversary of his father's death or that Father's Day was around the corner.

"Labor Day is a day for grilling out," Gerald said. "My dad and I loved more than anything to grill out together. We never missed a week during a single football season."

When I left for church Sunday morning, Gerald had begun assembling his new grill. When I got home later that afternoon, Lebron and Boston had joined him in the back yard of the Mission. The yard was L shaped. The long part went straight back to Nassau Street, on the other side of which a row of houses stood. Guys were always on the front porch of the house that faced us, drinking beer. A fence with barbed wire protected the backyard of the Mission. Gerald set up the grill on the short part of the L, closest to the Mission and away from Nassau Street.

I read a book and secretly watched Gerald. I watched him prepare the coals, then light them, then pour on so much lighter fluid the flames flew six feet in the air and Whiskers, the Mission's cat, almost jumped in my arms. Gerald turned and laughed at me and smiled, one front tooth and all. Then he began to put the meat on. He pulled out a plastic bag full of sauces and a brush. He pampered and softened the chicken breasts and steaks and ribs. He sat back and waited for them.

I put the book down and watched. Gerald sat with his hands folded in his lap. He glanced from one side of the yard to the other. The sun was bright and soft. The wind gently blew, and I knew it must have smelled like his father, the scent of charcoal and meat rubbing against the trees and through the grass and into his scruffy beard.

———

That night as I sat on my bunk bed with my back against the wall and my legs hanging over the side, I wrote in my journal:

"While others struggle in the privacy of their own homes, the homeless struggle on public display.

Who am I to know what homeless people need? How should I know? I huddle against the side of buildings and on benches and in my bunk bed at night and listen to them talk, and every one of their stories is different. The only thing their stories have in common is that when I listen, really listen, after the story is over, I always hear a still, small voice. It is the same voice. It does not care what I think about these people. It simply cares about the people.

Everyone has a right to a few things in this world, and one of those things is love. I don't know where the cutoff line to a home is, who is deserving and who isn't. Nor am I sure how we make those judgments for others, but collectively as a society we do. What if I judge why something happens to someone in order to pretend I can make sure it will never happen to me? What if it's equally or more important to understand why somebody thinks or behaves the way they do as it is for him or her to think or behave in ways I think are right?

We need shelter. But we need love, connection, and

belonging far more. Most people buy bigger homes in search of love, connection, and belonging, but in Gerald's pursuit—the memory of his father—he forfeited his home. I may not agree with Gerald's budget, but how dare I question his motives?

The German pastor and anti-Nazi dissident Dietrich Bonhoeffer described those who judge: 'Such people neither steal, nor murder, nor commit adultery, but do good according to their abilities. But…they must close their eyes and ears to the injustice around them. Only at the cost of self-deception can they keep their private blamelessness clean from the stains of responsible action in the world. In all they do, what they fail to do will not let them rest. They will either be destroyed by this unrest, or they will become the most hypocritical of all Pharisees.'"[12]

———

The next weekend Gerald grilled out again. It was a feast. He made steaks and ribs and hot dogs and baked potatoes with all the toppings. Enough to feed twenty-six. It was the best meal we ever had at the Mission, and four or five people even said thank you. Boston and Lebron sat outside with Gerald while he grilled. I ran next door to the Family Dollar to pick up aluminum trays. Gerald bought all the meat himself. "Gerald," I asked, "how much money did all of that cost?"

"I don't know, man. I didn't even look," he said.

I gave him a hug and offered to help pay. I told him I was going to write him a card. He told me I didn't need to.

"It's enough to know you're full and see a smile on your face," he replied.

At the Mission, homeless men fed other homeless men. When it was all over, Gerald took leftovers outside. Tim, The Good Samaritan Mission's cook, warned him, "If you feed people, they will come back looking for more." Gerald didn't care. He took a tray of spare ribs and hamburgers around the East Side neighborhood offering them to people.

This wasn't something homeless people, of all people, should do. They shouldn't cook for all their friends and people they just met and then take the leftovers to their neighbors. It didn't scream of responsibility or priorities. But it followed Jesus, who said "When having a feast, invite people who can never repay you."[13] That's what Gerald did.

A few mornings later, both Gerald and I overslept. By the time we got ready for work, everybody had already left. It was still dark outside. We crossed over Meeting Street wearing our work boots and jeans and T-shirts, walked behind the KFC, and took a left onto Line Street. We walked past a few abandoned houses and then one that wasn't, the lamp inside illuminating a shadowy red in the curtain.

Two guys walked up fast behind us, but when I checked my shoulder again they were gone. I almost stepped on the checkerboard belly of a dead snake. We continued down the sidewalk and veered off to the right, across a gravel lot. We were almost under the overpass of Highway 17 where a fifteen-year-old boy had been stabbed to death one morning only a few months before. Gerald extended his arm and put his hand on my chest. "Wait," he said.

My body was rigid, alert and nervous as a deer. We stood in the stillness for what felt like an eternity, feeling the morning air on our skin, listening to the droning sound coming from the overpass above. "What is it?" I whispered.

Gerald had his hand level with his forehead, peering deep into the darkness. Then he put it down. He started walking again. "Nothing," he said. "I just thought I heard something."

I can't explain the still, small voice. But when Gerald said, "I just thought I heard something," I felt it. My body tingled for a few seconds. I realized that love, connection, and belonging were more important to Gerald than having a home; and they were more important to me, too.

As we walked through the giant columns and the shadows of the overpass, I experienced a change in direction deep inside me. Living homeless was becoming a journey about more than myself or the homeless. It was about wanting a world to unlearn success in order to learn what matters more, purpose.

Chapter Twelve Questions:

1. The trappings of wealth can be a major distraction from finding purpose. In this story there is an association of wealth with morality, meaning those with wealth are of good character and those without wealth are of bad character. Do you see this in American culture? If yes, how does it affect our culture? How true is the correlation?

2. Have you ever thought you understood someone's problem when there was a much deeper problem behind the problem? What happened? How did that affect you? Could you relate to Gerald in any way in this story?

3. Consider the quote: "Such people neither steal, nor murder, nor commit adultery, but do good according to their abilities. But...they must close their eyes and ears to the injustice around them. Only at the cost of self-deception can they keep their private blamelessness clean from the stains of responsible action in the world. In all they do, what they fail to do will not let them rest. They will either be destroyed by this unrest, or they will become the most hypocritical of all Pharisees." How does this quote by the German pastor and anti-Nazi dissident Dietrich Bonhoeffer strike you? How do you think his usage of the words "responsible action" compares to our American culture's notion of being responsible?

4. I was humbled to see Gerald's understanding of feeding those "who cannot repay you." Have you ever seen yourself as superior to someone who in reality had a much more authentic understanding of what really matters? How did this affect you?

Chapter Thirteen
What It Takes to Survive

I learned a lot about what it takes to survive while living at The Good Samaritan Mission. Seeing the men struggle to survive showed me the dysfunction created by wants becoming needs.

I wrote in my journal:

"I can answer the question 'What do you really need to survive?' with simply 'God.' I can answer it by adding to God food, water, shelter, and clothing. I can add to that a vehicle, family, and a house. I can add to that not just any vehicle, but an SUV; not just any family, but one with a beautiful wife and two well-behaved children, preferably one boy and one girl; and not just any house, but a brick one in a safe neighborhood and a good school district.

I can simply say, 'I need as much as the people around me because my real need is their approval,' or 'maybe just a little more because my real need is to feel superior.' This means that what I need to survive changes depending on the place and time I was randomly born into.

Daily this question hides behind a corner and mugs me

THE DEFINITION OF SUCCESS

in the form of a commercial, finding out the income of a friend, or hearing about somebody's fantastic vacation. 'Put your hands up and give me all your joy!' it screams. Some days the question wins and makes off with my self-esteem and identity, dropping a calling card with a beautiful woman about to make love to a man with ripped abs on a beach far away with a perfect sunset every day, just for the two of them. I become sad and depressed. I'm sure no girl will ever want to marry me. My life will end living in a van down by the river. There is a tension between what I want and what I need. There is a force moving healthy 'wants' to unhealthy 'needs.'

Author and philosopher Alain De Botton, calls this 'Status Anxiety.' I call it success. Call it what you'd like, I think it is the dominant religion in western culture. Christianity is, at best, its side dish.

What I'm gaining from the Mission is not a clear understanding of a right or wrong answer but instead the insight that life is too short not to answer, 'What do I need to survive?' with authenticity. Is the answer literally, 'What do I need to survive?' If so, that's easy: protection from the elements and sustenance for my physical body. Or am I adding in things for other reasons? Rather than letting others tell me what I need to survive, I should have the courage to answer it for myself."

———

Frank was my bunkmate for the entire year I lived at The Good Samaritan Mission. Originally from Jacksonville,

Florida, Frank was forty years old. He was clean-cut. He had short brown hair and kind, light blue eyes. He was tall and broad-shouldered. He wore a green shirt with khakis and athletic shoes with white socks. He appeared as if he went to the doctor and the dentist regularly. He was in good shape. He attended some community college. More impressively, he was widely read. He was a speed-reader. He read philosophy. "Have you read Pascal?" he asked.

"No, Frank, I haven't read Pascal," I'd respond.

"Really?" he asked as if I had told him I had a third arm. "And you attended college? I can't believe they didn't teach you about Pascal."

I saw so much of myself in Frank. I saw my fears and struggles, my desire to be something important, my fear of failure. I felt if Frank and I had grown up in the same neighborhood as little kids, we would have been friends. I would have biked to his house after school. When I was scared to do something, he would admit he was too. We'd make each other feel better.

Frank was born an only child. His mother worked for the FBI. "She knew J. Edgar Hoover personally," Frank said. "She did an undercover case against the Klu Klux Klan," he added as if it was no more impressive than ordering a pizza.

Frank's father tragically died when Frank was very young. His father was a high-powered businessman and left the family in good financial standing. Frank's mother seemed like a good lady with good intentions who never meant to hurt Frank. Frank was all she had left. Add to that the dangers of the world she must have known from her occupation, and she never pushed Frank out the door. As a consequence, he didn't learn the things he needed to become independent.

Frank left home in his early to mid-thirties for the first time when he went to rehab. It started with the cops showing up to his makeshift party operation and drug store. Frank described those wild days as "a lot of people in and out of my mother's basement." I had a hard time seeing Frank being wild, but I could see him flipping out if he took drugs or had too much to drink. More concerning, I could see Frank being easily influenced by the wrong crowd and having a hard time saying no.

One night we were the last to finish brushing our teeth after curfew. I looked at the large mirror in the bathroom and saw Frank in the reflection. He stood at one of the other sinks. He wore his green shirt and khaki shorts with white socks and tennis shoes. Frank reminded me of the character Forrest Gump in ways: lovable, always taking life at face value, yet deeply thoughtful. Frank sporadically informed me of significant life accomplishments as if only announcing he had Cheerios for breakfast, like how he ran the fastest mile in the state of Florida when he was only in the ninth grade.

Frank finished brushing his teeth and looked at me. "I'm forty years old, Derek." And then after a small pause, "I should have a family and a career by now."

I looked at Frank. I tapped my toothbrush against the sink to shake the water. We stood in silence listening to the droning sound from the bathroom's fan. Frank waited with his hands at his side.

"Lots of people have both a career and a family at age forty," I said, "and wanting those things is perfectly normal. That's a normal way to feel, Frank." I didn't want to discount or undermine Frank's feelings. Frank straightened his back. He was rigid and looked as if he was hanging on my every word.

"Do you think a girl would ever be interested in me?" he asked. He took the smallest of steps backwards.

"I do, Frank," I said with sincerity.

"Are you sure?" He asked, stepping forward again. "Even while, you know, I'm living here? I've had girls lose interest after they found out where I lived."

"I have too, Frank," I admitted. "Yes, Frank, the right kind of girl will be interested in you for who you are and not because of where you live or what you do or how much money you make," I told him, or really the both of us.

"I'm thinking about getting on social media," Frank said. "Dollar Bill says it's a good way to meet women. The only thing is I want her to be a Christian, you know?" I had just shown Frank how to send his first e-mail the week before and wondered how he would set up accounts on social media.

"Frank, the thing is, you're waiting, right?"

"Yeah," he said.

"Well, while you're waiting you're learning things that are really important about life," I said. "Things like patience and perseverance. And you're growing the courage to keep trying, right?"

"Yeah, yeah, I guess I am," he said.

"Well, Frank, those are really important things to develop as a father and as a husband. When the time is right, if it's what God wills, you'll end up with those things."

While a lot of the other guys had families at some point, Frank wished for something he never had. He stood there, looking at me as if he so badly wanted to do something but didn't know what. He visibly wore his disappointment and the feeling he didn't measure up. I don't think he talked to many people about it, except the pastor and me. He bounced our words of advice off each other and then did nothing with them.

Frank had anxiety in groups and would lock up and not be able to start a conversation with anyone. He attended Alcoholics Anonymous. Being such a stand-up-looking guy, the entire time he flipped out in his mind he looked fine standing there alone—even confident. Frank so desperately wanted a relationship that he got into one or two that set him back.

Frank's career aspirations ranged from the medical field to wanting to get a horticulture degree to do high-end landscaping.

"The pastor says I should go back to school," Frank said.

"Oh yeah? What for?"

"Maybe the medical field. The pastor says people in the medical field make good money. Maybe I could be a nurse."

"That sounds great, Frank. When are you thinking about enrolling?"

"Well, I've got to go see the financial aid advisor and see what she says."

Weeks would go by. I would see Frank and ask, "Frank, have you gone to see the financial aid advisor?"

"No, not yet," he said. "I just don't think I'll be able to afford it."

For months I pushed Frank to go back to school. I didn't get it. Frank was clean-cut and sharp. He was smart. Going back to school was a normal thing. Lots of people did it. I didn't understand what Frank's problem was.

One day, though, Frank put me in my place. He was standing by his bed while I sat on my top bunk. He asked why I hadn't started the day labor agency I had been telling the guys I planned to start. I began telling him all the reasons. But Frank stopped me. He looked at me and said, "Derek, I don't get it."

I was offended. How dare he say that to me?

But Frank's reasons were really good. "Derek, you're clean-cut and sharp. You're smart. Starting a business is a normal thing. Lots of people do it."

Up to that point, Frank, to me, represented more than anyone the person who believed that things make each of us whole and without them we aren't really living. For Frank it was a career and a family. He felt like he could never achieve those things, and so he'd always live a life of being less-than.

It took humility to admit Frank and I were on the same playing field. We were both struggling with fears like failure, inadequacy, and what others would think of us. I realized we were in the same place. Sub out a career and family and sub in a successful company, book, or Harvard education, and I was in the same boat. I, too, felt like I didn't measure up. I, too, felt like sinking to the floor and hiding under the couch. I needed validation and approval to survive. Just like Frank.

———

I met Simon at the same time I was having these conversations with Frank. Only the conversation was very different.

Simon knew exactly what he needed to survive. It wasn't much. "I got a dictionary, a calculator, and a Bible—all the essentials for survival!" he exclaimed repeatedly. "Did you hear me? I got a dictionary, a calculator, and a Bible—all the essentials for survival!" He waived his arms and walked away from the Mission towards the AA building.

Simon was a large man with a large belly. He was six-foot-three and weighed two hundred and seventy-five pounds. He had a bald head and dark skin. He wore a dirty shirt and long dirty khaki pants and high-top sneakers. We often sat in white plastic chairs in front of The Good Samaritan Mission together.

"I'm waiting for my check to come in," Simon said. "I call them from a pay phone every day. 'Mr. Greene, Mr. Greene,' they say—"

"Who's Mr. Greene?" I interrupted.

Simon dropped his imaginary phone and glared. "That's me!" He picked his imaginary phone back up and continued the conversation. 'Calm down, Mr. Greene, please! Mr. Greene, Mr. Greene, please. Calm Down!" Then Simon demanded of whoever was on the other end of the line: "How am I supposed to calm down when I'm sleeping on a bench every night!?" Simon slept on the bench in front of Alcoholics Anonymous, which he attended, under a single florescent light across from The Good Samaritan Mission. Before bed he'd pace, taking each step with knees high and toes pointed up, as if crossing barbed wire, as if he were in the army or a marching band. Then one night, Simon acquired a key. After that, he'd let the moon settle and the doors lock, let the Mission's cat wander in and the cops drive by. He'd lay on the bench pretending to be asleep. Then he'd raise his head, make sure nobody else was looking, unlock the door, and pull the bench inside. I sometimes saw him the next morning, opening the Alcoholics Anonymous door, pulling his bench back out, brushing off his pants, making sure to leave before attendees arrived.

"Once my check comes in you won't see me no more," Simon said. "I'm going to get a place where I can have some peace and quiet."

"What does peace and quiet mean, Simon?" I asked.

"You know what it means," he said as if I asked how to add two plus two. "I'm going to sit in a chair like this." He put his arms behind his head and leaned back slightly in his chair. "Turn the radio on, and get some peace and quiet!"

It felt like Simon was only half there. He would shake a little when he walked. Simon and I prayed together every now and then.

"God, help me keep my drinking at bay," he'd start. "I drink thirty-two-ounce Cobras like an alcoholic," he'd confess. "Please help my check to come in," he'd conclude.

When I prayed, Simon typically decided he'd had

enough. "Please give us the strength..." I'd be saying when Simon would blurt out, "In Christ's name!" He pumped his fist into the air, stood up, and walked away.

"Well, I guess that's it," I'd say instead of amen.

One time, Simon asked me about my love life.

"Are you married?"

"No, Simon, I'm not married."

"Have you ever been married?"

"No, Simon, I've never been married."

Simon scrunched his eyebrows and formed a single wrinkle on his forehead.

"Do you have a girlfriend?"

"No, Simon, I don't have a girlfriend."

"Then you sleep with prostitutes?" he half asked and half concluded.

"No, Simon, I don't sleep with prostitutes." I ended up telling Simon I thought it was important to wait until you are married to have sex. Simon took it from there.

"You're a man!" he exclaimed. "You know why you're a man? Because you keep it in your pants." He stood up from his chair. "You're a double man," Simon continued. "You make me so happy I might not sleep with a prostitute tonight," he added, as if sex was a part of his evening routine as much as brushing his teeth. Simon left and began walking down the street. "That man back there thinks you should wait until you're married to have sex!" I heard him tell a stranger. "He's a man!" He pointed back at me without turning his body, marching down the street. "He's a double man!"

The stranger looked towards me. I sheepishly waved. The next time we prayed Simon included my future wife.

"Let him do what he was created to do," he asked God. "Do him like you did Adam, Father, and give him his Eve. Just don't let there be any apples around."

Simon never told me if he suffered from mental illness. I don't want to make light of his circumstances. But I can't even count the number of times he said, "All I need is a dictionary, a Bible, and a calculator!" I honestly wasn't quite sure what he meant. But it got me thinking because Simon was always upbeat. He never became very discouraged about his circumstances. He believed he had everything he needed.

Then one day Simon disappeared.

He came back one time to tell me he'd gotten a place where he could have some "peace and quiet." After that, I never saw him again.

———

Each man at the Mission had a different version of what he needed to survive. It was a moving target.

Zach worked as a carpenter before he got hit by a car while walking across the street, injuring his leg so that he couldn't work. When I first met him at the Mission, he didn't believe he could survive without a better leg. "It's just this thing with my leg," he told me.

Dale needed a driver's license. He couldn't get the job he wanted because it required one. Without it he felt like he couldn't survive. "I'm a master electrician," he said, "but not without a driver's license."

When Hal wasn't sleeping in front of the Family Dollar, he slept in front of Sherwin-Williams across the parking lot from Simon. I brought Hal granola bars and filled his water bottle and checked on him when it rained, but when I asked Hal, "What do you need?" he almost always told me, "A good woman and a hamburger."

For Frank it was a career and a family. He came in just before lights out when I brushed my teeth and said to me, "Derek, I'm not really living. I'm going on day after day, but I'm not really alive."

I thought the men at The Good Samaritan Mission would support each other more than they did. I expected them to be part of the same team with the same goal. But I found they bought into "Status Anxiety" just like me. They, too, divided amongst themselves.

"What does your job pay?" they asked each other openly. A guy who made twelve dollars an hour would make sure a guy making only ten dollars an hour knew it. That two dollars an hour difference added up to a little over four thousand dollars a year. But it felt like billions. I'll never forget when one of the men who graduated from a four-year university said to Frank, knowing Frank wanted to go back to school, "Well, excuse me for getting an education." He said it for no other reason than to validate himself and make Frank feel bad. I felt like punching him in the face or saying something cutting like, "So why are you here, buddy?"

And yet, his comment resembled the kind of comments I made on a regular basis—though more subtly—designed to carefully place me ahead of others in the pecking order, slightly higher on the ladder, slightly less likely to be thrown off the lifeboat first when the world gets low on rations.

———

I wrote in my journal:

"The Mission is changing how I look at and understand myself in relationship with others. The men look at my college degree and driver's license and vehicle the way I look at the founder of a billion-dollar company. I know in my heart I am no more or less important than any of the guys at the Mission; and because I know in my heart the men at the Mission are equal to me, that means the founder of a billion-dollar company is equal to me, too. I wonder why—if we're all equal—I don't pull for others more than I do?

It seems that if there is a God, this is all his or her responsibility anyways, to make sure we have food and water and the things we need to survive. God has to wake up the kittens in the morning. God has to pick the sun up to shine. God has to spin the earth on his or her finger like a basketball, and a bunch more planets after that, and moons around those planets, and an infinite number of universes after that. God also has to give the kittens milk. Kittens have to have milk. God has to create space and then somehow contain it. God has to make each snowflake different. God has to make babies giggle and keep them from eating too much dirt and watching too much TV. God has to tell each wave where to land and to do it over and over again. If there is a God, he or she has a lot to worry about, a lot to do so that we can survive; and, in comparison, all of us have very little to do to survive.

So what am I so worried about?

What if I think I need things like validation, approval, comfort, wealth, pleasure, security, productivity, power, expertise, education, health, sex, and even family when I really don't? What if putting great things like these first, ahead of purpose, deprives them of their greatness? What if I obsess over these things because I think they will somehow take care of me?

Some things I would have never seen from inside my bubble. Some things I have to unlearn in order to learn. Perhaps the biggest revelation is how truly dangerous putting things ahead of purpose can be. Isaiah, Jeremiah, and Ezekiel called things other than God that we think will somehow take care of us 'idols.'[14] They said idols make blind slaves of people and societies. They said that as idols increase in a society, things like morality, justice, mercy and care for 'the least of these' disappears. But had I continued to put idols ahead of purpose I would have spent my life believing I was being 'practical,' 'responsible,' and 'protecting my family.' My society calls this 'success.'"

———

Slowly, over time, Frank changed. "It was when I finally began giving everything to God" he says, "When I stopped focusing on what I did or didn't have," he added. "That's when I was able to take steps."

Frank eventually did go back to community college. He studied hard and decided over time it didn't make financial sense to continue. It didn't matter because he had already begun to mature, to see himself differently. He became less anxious and more joyful. He got a job working for a plumber making twelve dollars an hour, and at one point he told me he'd been sober for three years and had saved over ten thousand dollars.

One night I was in the bathroom brushing my teeth before bed. I looked up and saw Frank in the mirror. He stood in the doorway.

"Want to know one great thing about heaven?" Frank asked.

"Sure," I said.

"Okay. I'll tell you. There won't be any money in heaven," he said as if he had first-hand knowledge. "And God won't ask you, 'Where are you going to stay?'"

"And there won't be any money," he said again. "Not like here."

Chapter Thirteen Questions:

1. "Status anxiety," or "success," keeps us from our purpose in the world. To what degree does this affect you? How would the things you own, where you live, the things you strive for and say are important reflect or not reflect "Status Anxiety" or the pursuit of success?

2. Is it possible to be successful in the eyes of culture and completely miss the purpose for your life?

3. We can all take steps to release each other and ourselves from "Status Anxiety" and all the things we

think we need to survive. What are some steps you can take to release yourself from "Status Anxiety?" How can you take steps to release others?

Chapter Fourteen

James and Me

James and I were wired very differently, but what we had in common was neither of us registered for a dorm on time for Furman University's freshman class in 2004. Furman randomly put us together with another student, the three of us in a room designed for two. When I found out James would be my roommate, I called him up.

"James!" I found a picture of him online from his boarding school; he was wearing a blue blazer and glasses, sitting in front of a large book case. James had olive skin and dark hair with hazel eyes and a thin, fit build. "What kind of activities do you plan on doing at Furman?" I asked.

"I'm hoping to be on the mock trial team," he said. That sounded very official to me. "They had me come visit Furman to see if it's something I might be interested in before they offered me a scholarship."

Furman invited James for an official recruiting visit!? And a scholarship!?

"I'm thinking of majoring in political science. I'm planning to go to law school. How about you?" James asked.

"What are you planning to do at Furman?"

"Well, I'm coming because the basketball coach said if I can run a mile in five minutes and thirty seconds I can 'walk on' the team," I told James as if the life of my first born depended on it.

"Can you do it?" he asked.

"No," I said, "but I'm close. I'm training now and will keep training the first week of school before I have to run it the second week. I'm planning to run seven miles a day or so."

"Really? Well, if you want, I'll help you."

"What do you mean?" I asked.

"You know," James said, "I'll run with you."

I made the team. Then, early one morning a few weeks later James tapped me on the shoulder. My alarm had gone off at 5:15 a.m., but I didn't get up. It was 5:45 a.m. He leaned over his top bunk and said, "Derek, you need to get up or else you'll be late for practice," which started at 6 a.m. Had I kissed James it might have been a little weird, but it would have expressed how I felt.

After James helped me train to make the basketball team, we headed to the girls' freshman halls. We knocked on every door.

"Hi," I said. "My name is Derek, and this is James, and since we are freshman and y'all are freshman we thought we should introduce ourselves!"

James poked around the door and gave a smile and a wave. "Hi!" he said, "I'm James. How are you ladies this evening?"

I assumed I was the ladies' man of the two of us, but James put me in my place. After I obsessed over a girl all through my freshman year, I walked in at the beginning of sophomore year to find her and James kissing.

It actually made for a difficult situation. I knew how wonderful but demanding this girl could be. I took her to Zaxby's Chicken, a southern fast food restaurant, one time (classy, I know) but wasn't sure if it was a date or not. I concluded she didn't like me, only for her to tell me later on she did, but not anymore.

As we became friends, she did wonderfully amusing, but peculiar, things. Once, she called me eight times in a row. When I got out of my dentist appointment and called her back, she didn't respond for a week. She went through life pulling people's fire alarms.

Well, she pulled James's alarm hard.

"James," I said, "I know you're not going to believe me, but you should really think about this." I wasted my breath. We both had every reason to believe I might as well have told him, "I can't believe you pulled this off instead of me."

James bore the pain of the basketball team with me my freshman year, and I decided to do the same for him. It wasn't easy. We listened to Dashboard Confessional's "Screaming Infidelities" every morning when we woke up and every night before bed.

"Do we have to listen to this song over and over?" I asked.

"Yes. It makes me feel better," James said.

"Whatever."

Finally, one stormy Friday night James thundered into

our room. I was in bed. The lights were off. He stomped into the bathroom, flipped on the bathroom light, and flung the door shut. Then I heard an angry roar and a loud thud. James came out.

I sat up straight. "Are you okay?" I asked.

"I'm better now," he said.

The next morning, I got up to take a shower and found a hole punched in our bathroom wall. A few weeks later James inscribed on a note, "She wasn't worth it." He inserted it into the wall before patching it up. Finally, we had peace again.

———

I started giving James calls once I decided to start a day labor agency.

"I think we"—I used "we" early and often to help James see himself involved— "can start a temp agency that invests in employees by paying them more, coaching them, and helping them find permanent jobs," I said.

James listened. He asked a few questions.

"I think you should move down here and help," I said. "And I have great news: I already asked the pastor and he says you can stay at the Mission!" I added as if I were a telemarketer offering a special once-in-a-lifetime free vacation.

"I don't know that my parents will be too crazy about that," James said. After law school, James's mother intended for him to serve on the Supreme Court. "I've got this internship for an attorney I'm thinking about."

Hard as I tried, a few weeks later James still sat on the fence.

On September 23, 2009, I printed off papers to file with the South Carolina Secretary of State. I put them in an envelope with a check. I drove to the post office and sat next to the big mailbox with pickup later that afternoon. The engine ran. I felt the same anxiety I'd felt months earlier in front of my old apartment as I debated whether or not to move into The Good Samaritan Mission. "Dear God, please help us," I said. I pulled the mailbox cover down and stuck the envelope in.

That night I called James. "I went ahead and filed the papers with the Secretary of State." I paced in the backyard of the Mission. "If you want to help I'd love to have you, but if not, I'm going to try my best anyway."

Two weeks later I walked into the parking lot at The Good Samaritan Mission. There was James, wearing shorts and a t-shirt, sitting on the trunk of his car with a laundry bag full of clothes. I gave James a big hug.

"I didn't think I'd be here," he said.

"I'm glad you are," I responded.

I helped James get his things inside. I introduced him to the pastor and to the guys. I gave James a long walking tour of Charleston while we caught up on my time at the Mission and the master's degree he recently earned in Ghana. We walked through the College of Charleston, past the big fountain surrounded by grand oak trees and moss. The next morning, we woke up and started an adventure to get our first office open.

———

What do you do for a living?

I'm in med school.

I'm in law school.

I'm earning my MBA.

I'm a financial advisor.

I'm in medical device sales.

I'm a banker.

I'm in real estate.

All of these sounded like really good answers my Papa would have approved. James and I answered, "We live at The Good Samaritan Mission and work as carriage drivers. But don't worry, we're starting a nonprofit." What I felt like telling people was, "I don't fit in and I'm a loser. I'm sorry. Society rejects me. Will you please forgive me and let me eat crumbs from your table?"

One of the first meetings I set up was with Steve whom I'd met at a scholarship interview through my church a few years earlier. Steve was the CEO of Mattel who, among their other businesses, owned Fisher-Price Toys. When I first met him at the scholarship interview, he walked me out afterwards. When the committee asked me what I wanted to do with my life, I said, "I'm not really sure." Steve pinned me down in the hall. He told me, "Whatever you do, do it with all of your heart." He pointed his finger in my face. He really meant it. I didn't have a clue at the time who he was, but his intensity made me listen.

Steve met James and me at Barnes & Noble. I told him

about our plan to start the day labor agency we'd decided to name In Every Story.

"Why do you want to do that?" he asked.

"It can make a difference for a lot of people who need it," I said, "and it seems like what we should do."

"How much money do you think you'll need?" Steve wanted to know.

"I really don't know what we need money for," I said. "We just need to get started!" Steve laughed at that.

We talked for a while before he sat up straight with his chin resting in the palm of his hand. He looked at me and said, "You know, Derek, I've had only a couple of meetings like this in my life, less than a handful, maybe only three, and I believe your plans will succeed."

I asked Steve for three people's names he thought could help us, and one of them was Rick. Rick picked James and me up early one morning at the Piggly Wiggly across from The Good Samaritan Mission. He took us to breakfast. We drove down Meeting Street and small talked before ending up at Joseph's Diner where we sat at a table by the front window. Rick was a businessman, a consultant for the Governor of South Carolina, and had chaired the board for the local homeless shelter. He also wanted to know, "Why do you want to start IES?" We told him. He said, "My sense is that God is working through you."

Between these encouraging moments, everything else sucked. James and I didn't know what we were doing. We sat in our office, a study room at the College of Charleston. I Googled, "How to start a nonprofit temporary employment agency?" Nothing came up. I laid with my head on the table and prayed and pleaded with God. "Please, God, help us," I wrote over and over again in my journal. When I gave up on praying, I fell asleep. We met with insurance agents and attorneys and accountants. They didn't get it. They thought it was a one-in-a-million chance. So did we. People thought we were silly. So did we.

"Have you thought about going back to school?" they asked.

"Yes. Every day as a matter of fact," we replied.

"You know, you could get a real job and help out around the Mission on the weekends and just volunteer for a while," they said.

"I know, I know. I wish I could. Believe me, I wish I could," we'd each reply.

One day I said to James, "If we could ever employ just one person, I'd feel like we'd hit it big time."

Then one night in late October, James and I drove out to the local fair around 10 p.m. We had created a blog about In Every Story and wanted to snap a few pictures of Gerald for it while he worked through the day labor agency on the fair's cleanup crew. It was cold. We walked inside, past the rides and the food stands, past a small trailer that advertised "The World's Smallest Woman Inside!"

"He's about this tall," I said to a man in an orange vest, straightening my hand to the side, almost at eye level. "Black guy, about 50 or so, one front tooth."

"He got a kind of gray beard?" The man asked.

"Yeah, yeah, have you seen him?"

"I think so. He's over there by the teriyaki chicken and the caramel apples. That's his section," the man said, pointing back in the direction we'd come.

"Over that way?" I asked, second guessing the man.

"Yeah, over there. You'll see him."

James and I walked back but couldn't find Gerald. Then we split up and went separate ways. Ten minutes later, my phone rang. "I found him," James said, "over by the agricultural building."

James and I sat down and waited until Gerald got a break.

"What do you think it would be like to be the World's Smallest Woman, anyways?" I asked James. "Having people come look at you and gawk while others stay outside, too horrified and uncomfortable to look." I sat there with my hands in my pockets, feeling the fuzz of my jacket and the cold between my toes. "It would be dehumanizing, wouldn't it? Having people on the other side of the glass while you're in a bubble?"

"Yeah, it would. And who knows what you get paid," James said.

In front of us stood a man wearing a baseball cap. The man had shuffled Gerald inside to sweep some more. "Do you work for the fair?" I asked.

His cheeks were large and rosy and he wore a big burly jacket. "No, I'm a member of…" and then he said the name of a nonprofit charity.

"Oh, okay," I said.

"We volunteer our time," the kind man continued. "You

know, all the profits and proceeds of the fair go towards charities and scholarships." The way the man said it let me know he expected to be congratulated.

"Oh wow, that's great!" I said. I turned to James and added, "That's pretty cool," making sure the man could hear.

When Gerald came out he looked tired. He wore a baseball cap with sunglasses on top, jeans, a white t-shirt, and a light green jacket. "Hey guys, how you doing?" We shook hands. "We need to make this quick" he said, still holding his dust pan and broom. We snapped a few pictures.

"Can we do anything for you?" James asked. Gerald needed to call the night watchmen from one of our phones. He also wanted a lemonade. "How was the night?" James asked.

"It's been quiet," Gerald said, "but a long and frustrating day of waiting. I got to the agency at 6 a.m. but didn't get any work until late this afternoon."

I walked away from James and Gerald and towards the lemonade stand. "Extra sugar!" Gerald hollered.

"You won't get sick from too much, will you Gerald?" I asked, thinking of Gerald's diabetes, still walking towards the stand.

"Naw, man, I'm good to go. I've been walking around all night."

We gave Gerald his lemonade and chatted for a few minutes more before he said, "Okay, guys, I need to get back to work." We shook hands again and turned to go.

As we walked, James said, "Derek, that lemonade you

just bought Gerald cost almost as much as he makes in an hour at minimum wage, seven dollars and twenty-five cents." James pulled out his phone to use as a calculator. "Even if Gerald got six hours every day, in a twenty-two-day work month that's nine hundred and fifty-seven dollars monthly, before taxes and before paying five dollars a day for transportation to and from work through the agency, the cost of any equipment, and the cost to cash his check." When James factored in the time Gerald had waited, to the time he'd left for the fair around 4 p.m., to the time he finally began getting paid at 5 p.m., to the time he got back around midnight, Gerald was making less than two dollars an hour.

"Yeah," I added, "I worry Gerald will never make it out of homelessness, between his back pain, his diabetes, and the way he stumbles out of the Mission to work every morning holding his chest."

James and I walked past the families with strollers and the teenagers smoking cigarettes, past the fenced in area where local news stations broadcast from the fair, past the American flags, past the group of young adults wearing shirts with the name of their church on them. We walked past the slides with the children at the top, bright eyed and innocent. A child came down the slide with her hands in the air, the world at her fingertips.

Walking through the fair, past the families, the church youth groups, and the American flags, I mourned my society—a society I am part of and responsible for that missed it so badly, that even while a man suffered directly in front of it could enjoy the fruit of his labor while bragging about how it put on a fair to raise money for charities and scholarships.

I wondered, what could blind us so badly? I believed that Gerald and the homeless, and those who suffer from a fragmented and segregated society, are behind a glass similar to the one that makes objects of the World's Smallest Woman at the fair—a societal glass put up collectively in the name of success.

Even if I didn't explicitly think this way, I bought into a system where the more those who were different from me were seen as threats to my success, the less I wanted them around. And the less they were around, the more I saw them as threats.

Jesus said, in the Sermon on the Mount, that I cannot love God and money. But the word he used for money, *mammon*, meant the use of money in a systematic way. Mammon represented the system.

He next said, "That is why I tell you do not worry." It's as if Jesus knew every culture's system would perpetuate worry and fear, keeping us from one another and steering us towards lives of success instead of purpose. It's as if he could anticipate the things people would hear if they started whispering that they wanted out of their culture's system. They would hear things like "be practical," and "be responsible," and "get a real job and volunteer on the weekends." Being practical and volunteering on the weekends aren't bad; those things aren't necessarily the problem. The problem is what I believed was the subtle message behind it—to love mammon, or the system, first.

As my definition of success changed to a life of purpose, I noticed a few things: Growing up in the culture of my middle- to upper-class town had left me cripplingly isolated. I struggled to grasp things like forgiveness and hope. I carried unnecessary stress and bondage from untrue fears and judgements. I realized that telling others to "be practical" and "be responsible" were ways I told them to worry and to fall in line with the system. In essence, I, too, told them to love mammon first.

I realized it couldn't be only Gerald and the poor who were oppressed because free people would not walk past Gerald at the fair and do nothing. Free people would go to any lengths necessary to free others. It was nearly impossible to see, and even harder to admit, that even as I lived in "the land of the free," I was oppressed and enslaved. Suddenly, I understood what Jesus meant when, before talking about mammon, he said, "If the light you think you have is actually darkness, how deep that darkness is!"

In that moment, I felt that I needed someone free to free me. How could one slave free another? How could I, as a slave, see clearly to address the burdens of others and, in a wider scope, our larger societal problems?

In general, I did not see how the American Christianity I grew up in loved mammon any more or less than the rest of society. There seemed to be a deep symbiotic relationship between American Christianity and mammon. Take, for example, these words from Reinhold Niebuhr: "All responsibility for the community, for the safety of loved ones, for the preservation of civilization, is disallowed for the sake of the individual's perfection…."[15] It sounds like he's talking about success. But he isn't. Niebuhr, a theologian, is talking about Christianity's version of success based on "competitive righteousness."[16]

From my vantage point, American Christianity encouraged its followers to be a double success. On Sundays it offered success as "an instrument of competitive righteousness." Through the week, churchgoers became "practical" and "responsible" to serve the system and mammon in turn. It was exhausting. People appeared worn out and weary from the effort. It's bad enough to be oppressed by one form of success, but two!? With that observation, I saw American Christianity doing almost no good even as it insisted that it served God. The world laughed, quietly grieved, and started looking for hope in other places.

However, my journey surrounding my time at The Good Samaritan Mission cut like a sword; it separated Jesus from success and the failure of American Christianity and people like me—Jesus became the savior both from success and American Christianity. I felt "like a burning stick that has been snatched from the fire."[17] I began to believe in Jesus even as I began to hate success and American Christianity.

In the year I lived homeless, I realized that no human was my enemy. Not those I had feared or judged, nor those who others labeled as the oppressors. My enemy wasn't the Republicans or Democrats, Muslims or Christians or atheists, blacks or whites or Hispanics, the rich or poor. I could stare into every human's eyes hard enough to see something of God and myself in them.[18] But I had a very real enemy I'd previously ignored. It was an evil that, through secular and religious success, divided American brothers and sisters, and all of humanity, so that all were oppressed.

———

On November 3, 2009, I wrote in my journal:

"I can be distracted with many different things, but at the end of the day my heart wants purpose. 'But I gave you success. I gave you approval and pleasure and comfort and security and success,' I'll say to my heart.

'You ignored purpose, the only thing I asked for, and gave me those other things instead!' my heart will respond.

I have great moments of joy and great moments of pain. My joy and pain come from the same reason: by choosing purpose, I'm choosing an alternative source of approval other than 'status anxiety' or success. And even though I'm not choosing 'status anxiety' or success, I still feel them pulling at me.

I want purpose. But I'm beginning to believe it wants me far more than I could ever want it. Purpose loves me and loves others; it wants to help through me. It whispers to my heart from birth to death. It isn't logical or provable and requires action in the face of uncertainty. But I must listen to it to live a fulfilling life. I want to rid myself of 'status anxiety,' let go of success, and fully commit to my purpose."

———

Some days James and I ran down Columbus Street together, up and over the Ravenel Bridge and back. But once, I ran the bridge alone.

When I got to the top, I stopped. I held the railing with both hands and looked out over the harbor. I looked at the church steeples, the cranes moving containers on and off ships, a pelican diving into the water close to Drum Island.

My thoughts raced: I need a break from this constant uncertainty, a cold beer or a normal job my Papa and everybody else would approve of. My heart remembered the promise it made in Kenya. "If you give me something meaningful and purposeful to do with my life, I won't quit until you say it is time to quit or until it is complete," I whispered to myself.

I began walking again, slowly across the bridge towards Mt. Pleasant. I thought of my grandmother. She had wanted to be a nurse her entire life. She was in her late seventies and still thought about going to school to become one, and it made her sad she had never tried. I could see how keeping a healthy desire pent up for an entire life could hurt a person and those around them. I thought about Moses, my favorite kindergartener in Kenya. He was full of energy and bright and smart. A few months after I got back I learned he had stomach cancer and died.

Then I thought about Frank. After Frank put me in my place, I realized we struggled with the same fears of failure, inadequacy, and what others would think of us. I wondered if showing Frank how to move forward might be more effective than telling Frank. I had to do this, not just to help men at the Mission, like Frank, have better jobs but so that Frank could see how to move forward on his own.

I'm sure I looked to others passing by as if I was in pain. I was. Finally, I said out loud, "Okay God, I don't care if this thing kills me or if I end up alone and homeless living in a van down by the river. I'm going to trust you and go for it. I'm going to jump. I'm going to start In Every Story." I jumped forward—a symbol of purpose.

————

Deciding to jump can be embarrassing. I gave speeches around town to build momentum for IES, and I cried every time. I cried because I knew we were doing the right thing. I'd get towards the end and be so overcome with gratitude we'd made it this far—even though we hadn't even opened an office yet, in faith I could see we had made it already, we were already there, with hundreds of branches across the country—and in gratitude I'd start crying.

I most clearly remember the time we were at Charleston Southern University.

James and I read somewhere about a guy who sent one hundred letters to people who could help him start a non-profit and it worked, so we thought we'd do the same. We sent one hundred letters to local groups and companies we thought could help, and the only one to respond was Charleston Southern University. We got a call from Dr. Allen who asked if we could do a presentation on In Every

Story for a group of leaders on campus. "Sure we could," James and I said. We spent weeks putting together a PowerPoint presentation and one morning headed to Charleston Southern.

"Hi, my name is Derek Snook and this is James DeCamilla," I addressed the audience as if I was introducing the CEO and vice president of a major corporation. "We are both voluntarily living at The Good Samaritan Mission which is a halfway house for the homeless. It's a dorm room with twenty-six beds and each bed has a locker." The audience looked back at us like we were insane.

About twenty-five campus leaders were there to hear our presentation. We told them about day labor. We explained how In Every Story was different and how it invested into its employees. We told them about Frank and Gerald and how we believed In Every Story could benefit them.

At the end, I tried to tell them, "Every good story has conflict, but it also has examples of God's love…" I started choking and tearing up. I thought about Gerald, and Frank, and Dollar Bill, and Walter, and the other guys. I also longed for a society that placed purpose above success. I wanted to finish my sentence by saying, "…God's love, hope, and redemption." But I couldn't.

James knew his cue. "What Derek's trying to say is…" he chimed in as he stood up and finished. The folks at CSU were kind and patient and thoughtful and gave us their full attention.

But that's not what made it my favorite talk. What made it my favorite talk was when Dr. Allen asked a bald man who wore a very tight shirt on very big biceps to pray for us. He must have been the football or strength coach.

I wasn't particularly paying attention. I wiped my nose and my eyes.

Then I heard, "God, help James and Derek to crush them! Crush the enemy!" He was referring to our competitors. "Crush them!" he emphasized again. He pounded his fist into the palm of his hand. His face turned red. I thought his muscles would explode and his shirt would tear in half and a large, green superhero would emerge.

James and I could hardly restrain ourselves. I left ready to charge the gates of hell with a squirt gun. We had no sooner exited the building before James shared an impersonation which he would do spontaneously for months to come. "Crush them!" James yelled, pounding his fist into the palm of his hand. "Rawr!" James roared like a mighty lion.

The experience showed me that James and I were not alone in our dream for a better society, one that put purpose first and rid itself of success. In fact, among some there existed a raw hunger.

———

That night James and I walked down King Street to play a game of pool at C.J.'s Bar. It's a dark bar with a row of booths and two pool tables. We drank Yeungling, James's favorite, for two dollars each during happy hour. James set up the rack and took the break shot.

"You know, James, putting purpose ahead of success and

starting IES is helping me see other things I didn't like before in a better light."

"Oh yeah?" James asked. "Like what?"

"Well," I said, "like rejection and failure."

"I can't wait to hear about this," James chuckled.

"Well," I gathered my breath as if I might deliver the Gettysburg Address, "what if I told you I know a secret tool to build your character and teach you virtues like perseverance and patience? And what if it showed you what was most important in life? What if it made you stronger and built your identity in the things that matter the most? What if it gave you gratitude for the things you have and increased your gratitude when you got what you wanted? Most people would sign up for that, including me and you, right?"

"Right," James said.

"Well," I continued, "when you put purpose ahead of success in your life, that's exactly what rejection and failure do for you. When you put purpose first in your life, rejection and failure teach you to persevere and have patience. They affirm that your purpose is important because if not, you'll quit. They focus your purpose on solid and not superficial things. And they increase your gratitude when you get what you want! When you put purpose first the rejection and failure just make you stronger."

"I'd never really thought about it like that," James said. By this time James was beating me pretty good and was ready for another Yeungling. "I can see what you're saying," he said, "purpose can give meaning to even rejection and failure."

"It can," I said. "You know, if Jesus came from heaven to earth to walk in our shoes and faced rejection and failure even to the point of death, he must have had a strong sense of purpose to do that."

James had one ball and then the eight ball left. "Corner pocket. I'll give you a chance to experience failure and rejection," he said, leaning over the table with his eyes focused on the cue ball. James smiled at me. "Good game. Want to play again?"

We walked down King Street back to The Good Samaritan Mission. Just as we reached the Mission, James asked, "If that's true about Jesus, I wonder why someone would go to such lengths?"

I prayed that night on the top bunk in a room with twenty-five other homeless men for all the things I didn't have. Then I said thank you for what I did. I had a project and a way to help others. I had a community of unconditional love. I had a deep internal conversation with an external guide. I would fall off course many times, but I realized those things would drive me and give me purpose, and that I would never again need success.

Chapter Fourteen Questions:

1. Not knowing where to start was a challenge for me and James. Have you ever not known where to start in pursuing your purpose? What's the smallest step you can take?

2. "Gerald and the homeless, and those who suffer from a fragmented and segregated society, are behind a similar glass as one that makes objects of the World's Smallest Woman at the fair, a societal glass put up collectively in the name of success." What do you think about this?

3. "I want to rid myself of 'status anxiety,' let go of success, and fully commit to my purpose." Do you experience this? What, if anything, is keeping you from committing to your purpose?

4. "The experience showed me that James and I were not alone in our dream for a better society that put purpose first and rid itself of success. In fact, among some there existed a raw hunger." What do you think about this? Is there a desire in our society among some to be rid of success?

5. I talked about how rejection and failure are critical to pursuing the purpose for our lives. How did you feel about this? What rejection and failure have you already faced? What rejection and failure do you need to face?

Epilogue

Next Steps

A few months later, James and I drove across the country to visit existing models similar to what In Every Story eventually became. The journey led us to the bottom of the Grand Canyon, to camping on the Pacific Ocean, and to me walking around in the snow in Glacier Park wearing a T-shirt and shorts. We returned in a different vehicle than the one we started in. This adventure deserves a book of its own.

In March of 2011, I opened our first In Every Story (IES Labor Services) office in downtown Charleston, directly in front of The Good Samaritan Mission. By 2014, IES employed more than 150 employees on a daily basis, donated and rewarded hundreds of thousands of dollars, and helped more than one hundred employees find permanent jobs. While I am still a part owner of IES Labor Services today, the company is pressing forward to bigger and better things without my involvement in an active leadership capacity.

Purpose, in my view, is the ongoing process of three essential ingredients.[19] The first is self-abandonment through helping others (best when a set project). The second is a community of unconditional love. The third is having a guide. James and I began working on In Every Story, a decision that required self-abandonment, to pursue a set project that would help others. We had a community of unconditional love with each other, the men at The Good Samaritan Mission, and a small group of friends and family who supported us. We had a deep internal relationship with an external guide. We had purpose.

Some may ask, "Are you saying we all need to live among the homeless?" or "How does this apply to having a family?" I, too, have asked these same questions. They do not have easy answers. But I believe that if your biggest concerns are questions like these, then you're hardly concerned enough.

Adopting purpose as the lens through which we live our lives, while removing the culture-fed idea of success, is the real challenge. It requires a change of heart. Weighing my experience living homeless against my experience undergoing heart change, I can say that changing a heart is a much harder task. Not kept in check, my heart soon became consumed with its own success, one of self-righteousness and pride in my charity. Heart change is ongoing work.

Because it is a matter of the heart and not of circumstance, purpose can and will look different for each of us. But it always leads through death to life.

I experienced this mysterious truth in many ways. These are a few:

I experienced it in my individual actions. I thought putting purpose first would mean losing approval and status, possibly even my physical life. Instead, I found that the greatest joy in life is to die for what I truly believe in long before I take my last breath.

I experienced it in my vocation. I thought putting purpose first would be an abandonment of a successful career. Instead, I realized how success could demand my every life decision, even my choice of occupation. Purpose drove me to quit a job making three times as much money to take one at minimum wage. Eventually, purpose led me to a better vocation than I could have imagined.

I experienced it in my relationships. I thought putting purpose first would leave me lonely with people I couldn't relate to. Instead, I saw how success had caused me to view as unequal those different from me in race, class, or belief system. Purpose neither judged me nor let me stay where I was. It pushed me to seek to understand. In turn, I developed rich relationships and learned about life from the men at The Good Samaritan Mission. I began to understand how much less I knew than I initially thought.

It played out in how I see society. In my opinion, individual responsibility, charity, and government programs mean little while an evil divides our society. They mean little while all live in bondage to success and struggle to find purpose. Through my experience I saw how purpose was key to society's biggest problems. Through purpose the men at the Mission and I found life by helping set each other free on equal terms. We loved each other as we loved ourselves.

I believe our society needs defragmentation and integration across race, socioeconomic status, and belief systems. This will seem to some as death, but I believe it will lead to life. By creating opportunities for empathy— voluntarily abandoning one's strength for others' weakness—we as individuals and as a society will find purpose through fulfilling the needs of one another, purpose that we need to live and thrive. When we truly see one another's pain, we will want to help.

I fear that continuing with the status quo of keeping success the priority will continue to damage our society. I fear the status quo will stress it to the point of collapse. I find it curious how an individualistic society seems to produce individuals who are so often blind to their individual responsibilities to that society. I have much more to say on these matters, but this will have to suffice for now.

———

I have learned that purpose, in time, may bring the things of success. But when they come they matter less because a life of purpose is enough.

And yet, though I believe this is true, I fail at taking my own advice. During this year of homelessness, I believed the truth of purpose even as I continually failed at it. I also felt a loving presence in those I encountered along the way. These two things together convinced me to follow Jesus.

I buy the whole crazy story, most of the time. And it is a crazy story. I believe Jesus came to earth as God in human form to walk in our shoes and empathize with us all. I believe he lived a perfect life of putting purpose ahead of success and that it lead to his death. I believe he rose from and conquered death for us all. Because of Jesus, I believe each of our pursuits of purpose must go through—and not avoid— death to life.

"To what extent must my life change?" I believe that's the wrong question. "To what degree must I cast off being 'practical' and 'responsible'?" I believe that, too, is the wrong question. According to Jesus, no amount of change is enough, and those who try to draw lines around what is or is not enough love themselves more than God or others.

In my view, the American Christian church as a whole is irrelevant in today's society. I believe it is in general a hypocritical supporter of success. I believe that in general it is systematically failing our nation. It's a negative reinforcing cycle between congregants and leaders. Every member of the American Christian Church, counting myself first, shares blame. I believe America has an idol of success, and one of its most faithful worshipers, if not the most faithful, is American Christianity. I believe this explains how subscribers of American Christianity think, live, and vote.

I worry that American Christianity's hypocrisy will perpetuate an already emerging internal persecution and ultimately lead to a backlash of external persecution. I say this in the context of the dream I had of hell as a child from chapter one.

In one image, a man stood against a brick wall with his legs spread while other men shot guns at him. In the other image, Christians ran in fear through a ripe corn field toward a church. Here's the thing: nobody was chasing the Christians. In the context of my dream, this social upheaval happened not because of provocation, but because of a voluntary persecution and seclusion from the rest of society. In the reality of today, I see this manifested in how many Christians silo and bubble off in society. This silo-ing doesn't just happen in a social context but extends into industries, too, like music, books, movies and more. In doing so, they forego the opportunity to fill a needed role in society and instead seek shallow approval from others living within the same fearful bubble.

What's more, I believe the Christians in my dream should have been running towards the man, not away. The example of Jesus teaches that life can only be found by courageously standing between the men who were shooting and the man being shot at. Doing so would have protected that man, their society, and, in the long run, themselves. They did not. Society eroded. My dream ended.

Today I see this same fearful approach to living in how American Christianity seems to believe Jesus died so we could "practically" and "responsibly" avoid death. I hear this in the constant admonition from people who say that "when I have children" I will be more "practical" and "responsible." I do not have children. They may be right. But I believe Jesus died so that through him I could face and conquer death, not avoid it. I want to live a long, happy life with a family, but a life of purpose is what's worth living and, if need be, dying for.

Despite American Christianity's failures, I believe our

country's ever-growing lack of and need for purpose still requires Jesus. I believe that Americans are beginning to find Jesus not because of American Christianity but in spite of it. I believe the group who finds and believes in Jesus is beginning to reinvent itself. I believe that if Jesus is real, and you want purpose, then he's drawing you to Him.

———

Putting purpose first is the ongoing struggle in my life. I feel just what the Greek philosophers described: I'm always driving a chariot with two horses, each headed in opposite directions.

Even as I wrote this book, the majority of my thoughts were about quitting and doing something to make money. For periods of time, I did. "Nobody will ever read this," I'd tell myself. "And women don't marry unemployed men," I'd rub in. "I'm getting a job and posting an online dating profile," I'd conclude.

Making the pursuit of purpose primary in my life means I am often a stranger and outcast in society. I feel this at times even among those I care for and love. But I can't deny what I believe: What I spend my time on is what I implicitly believe is worth dying for. I believe purpose is worth dying for. I believe I find life by giving my life so that others may live.

For the first part of 2017, I lived in a poor neighborhood in Pittsburgh, Pennsylvania. The first week I went for a walk, and while talking to a close friend on the phone, a young black male in a black hoodie and black pants walked out of a public housing unit. In the doorway stood another male, much bigger and in a white T-shirt, who looked at me. I walked a little faster, peeking over my left shoulder. I didn't even hear what my friend said as he poured his heart out over the phone.

Two blocks to the right, down Allendale Street, is an African Methodist Episcopal church. I attended church there on a regular basis.

That Sunday, two young males, one with dark skin and the other with light skin, sat in the front left of the church. They wore a black and a gray hoodie respectively.

Later that night I drove to Chartiers Avenue, the main street that runs through our small, poor borough. I was on my way to watch the Super Bowl in a bar. As I walked to the bar from my parked vehicle, I saw the same two young males from church approaching. They were wearing their same hoodies. I didn't grab my wallet. I didn't look around to see who was nearby.

When I saw them both at church the following Sunday I struck up a conversation with Greg, one of the two young men. "Yeah, man," he told me, "I live on the other side of town but wanted to come over here to see what the church was like, you know?"

The next Sunday at 2 p.m., one block behind my church, two young black males were shot by a third. The suspect ran in a black hoodie towards Chartiers Avenue, the same street on which I'd seen Greg and his friend the week before.

The news reminded me of a conversation I had with my good friend Jay in Charleston a few months earlier. Jay dreamed out loud about living in a poor neighborhood half a mile from where he ran his construction company. He wanted to be closer to his employees. He wanted to reduce income inequality. He wanted to do something that matters. "I could get my wife to do it," he said, "if somebody could promise her son would not be in danger."

When the shooting happened in my poor neighborhood in Pittsburgh, three blocks down on the same road a close friend had driven through on her way home forty-eight hours earlier, I immediately shamed myself for risking her life by living here. I thought, we can't be sure it's safe; let's go somewhere we can be sure. Then I reminded myself how purpose, like Jesus, requires acting in faith in lieu of certainty. I said to myself what I said to Jay a few months earlier, referring to the idea that Jesus is God's son and came to earth and died and rose again: "Danger is a possibility, but what if God had taken that same approach?"

The next time I saw my pastor, I asked him about the shooting. For him, it was nothing new.

"It's the young ones," he said, "between the ages of fifteen and nineteen. They are the dangerous ones. They are the ones that shoot each other." He stood at the front of his church, spreading his arms with his palms down as if resting on a casket. "I've buried young men right here," he said with the weight of a man who has learned to bear a broken heart.

"Why do they shoot each other?" I wanted to know. Partly I cared, but mostly I worried I would get shot. Am I safe? Can I live in this neighborhood? The same thoughts raced through my head as years earlier when I sat in my truck, gripping the steering wheel with sweaty palms, before moving into The Good Samaritan Mission.

My pastor paused but not for long. "You know what it is, Derek? I think at its core is a need for legitimacy. These young men are so overlooked, so devalued, so beat down, they have such a gaping hole in their hearts for belonging that when someone steps on their Jordan's or says something about their girlfriend or their sister, it's easy for them to explode. Underneath it all is a need for legitimacy."

Oh, I thought. I felt my own need for legitimacy. I realized that need for legitimacy found false, violent expression through shooting someone just as much as ripping them off or being indifferent to their existence and suffering. I realized I needed to empathize with young men in hoodies in spite of my fear, for their well-being, for my well-being, and for society's well-being. I hoped that together we could find purpose by helping fulfill each other's needs. I hoped we could heal and both be set free.

Isn't the tension Jay and I experienced, the desire for purpose confronted by our fears and worries and success, reflected in our daily lives? Isn't it reflected in our vocations? Isn't it reflected in our relationships? Isn't it reflected in where we choose to live? Isn't it reflected in our broader debates and societal structure? Isn't it easier to revert both as individuals and as a society to success and let it become the driving force for these debates instead of purpose?

I challenge you to deeply consider: What is purpose? What does it require of you? How does purpose apply to your life? How does purpose apply to your individual actions? To your vocation? To your relationships? And how does purpose apply to how you see society? What things do you need to unlearn in order to learn about purpose?

Answering how purpose plays out in our lives and society is *the* challenge we face today. It will have a high cost and be messy. But neglecting the question will be costlier and messier. A life of purpose is a life worth living. Whether conscious or not, the way we live answers what each of us thinks about purpose and success. We are already choosing one. I hope you'll join me in putting purpose first.

We would love to join you on your path to pursuing purpose. Here are things you can do:

1) Visit and sign up for our email list at dereksnook.net where you'll find our blog and a range of free resources to keep you inspired.

2) Leave a review on Amazon to help others know if they should read this book. What you have to say has even more power than you think it does!

Tell others! Does your story look different to you after reading this book? Tag us on Instagram @dereksnook_ and Facebook @derekcsnook using the hashtag #purposeoversuccess to tell us about how you're living a life of #purposeoversuccess and how you see #purposeoversuccess in the lives of others. We've also created a Facebook profile frame (search on Facebook for the #purposeoversuccess profile frame) as an easy way to invite others into the conversation of living a life of #purposeoversuccess.

Acknowledgments

Thank you Nic, Mike, and Tay for letting me finish this book on your sailboat in New York City. Thank you Alison, Mary, and the gang at Glazed Doughnuts on King Street in Charleston, South Carolina. Your love, iced coffee, and maple bacon doughnuts kept the writing going. Thank you to the many people who reviewed this manuscript and provided valuable feedback in the form of conference calls. Many of you went to extensive lengths; and for that, I can't say thank you enough. These people include: Doug Fotia, David Plant, Anna Nodtvedt, Brad Dunson, Julie Cabezas, Frank Burwell, Graham Allcott, Bucky Buchanan, Kim Sutton, Chad Miller, Marina Hart, Nic van Vliet, Jason Moore, Brandon Flanagan, Mario Nardone, Robyn Green, Scott Parnell, Emily Wilson, Celestee Roufs, Mary Pan, Zoe Schlag, Sarah Saxton-Frump, Beth Jackson, Alexis Hall, Sue Pellum Sanders, Melissa Cote, and Lauren Chafin.

Thank you Jamie Wiggan for letting me keep you up late at night reading you chapters, insisting, "You have to hear this one because it's the best!" only to completely rewrite it again the next day.

Thank you to Jack Hoey and the team at IES. This book would not have been possible without you.

Thank you Brittany Jones. Your patience, loving support, encouragement, and own pursuit of purpose helped me stay the course.

Thank you Cinelle Barnes and Julie Rosenau. You helped make this book the best it could be and pushed me to write better in spite of my complaining.

Thank you to my family for your love and support.

Thank you to the many characters in this book. Thank you to James, who endured far more than readers know in helping get In Every Story started. Thank you to the men I met while at The Good Samaritan Mission. You showed me that no matter our struggle, nothing can separate us from purpose.

References

[1] Viktor Frankl, *Man's Search for Meaning;* Donald Miller's summary of Viktor Frankl's work; and the story in this book influenced this definition.

[2] Luke 10:27

[3] Matthew 7:20-22

[4] C.S. Lewis, *Mere Christianity* (Samizdat, 2014), 38.

[5] Luke 10:38-42

[6] Matthew 20: 16

[7] Jane Jacobs, *Death and Life of Great American Cities* (New York: Modern Library, 2011), 182.

[8] Mohandas K. Gandhi, *My Experiments with Truth: An Autobiography.*

[9] Matthew 25: 40

[10] Frederick J. Schumacher, *For All the Saints: A Prayer Book for and by the Church*, (Delhi: American Lutheran Publicity Bureau, 1994), 959.

[11] Paraphrase inspired by several different quotes by Henry David Thoreau, *Walden.*

[12] Eric Metaxas, *Bonhoeffer: Pastor, Martyr, Prophet, Spy,* (New York: Thomas Nelson, 2011), 470.

[13] Luke 14: 12-14

[14] Books of the Old Testament

[15] Frederick J. Schumacher, *For All the Saints: A Prayer Book for and by the Church*, (Delhi: American Lutheran Publicity Bureau, 1994), 959.

[16] Ibid.

[17] Zechariah 3: 2

[18] Inspired by several different quotes by Martin Luther King, Jr.

[19] Viktor Frankl, *Man's Search for Meaning;* Donald Miller's summary of Viktor Frankl's work; and the story in this book influenced this definition.

41528048R00109

Made in the USA
Middletown, DE
07 April 2019